AQUACULTURE ACTIVITIES IN AFRICA

By

Joshua Kamya Kigeya

Order this book online at www.trafford.com
or email orders@trafford.com

Most Trafford titles are also available at major online book retailers.

Printed in the United States of America.

ISBN: 978-1-4669-4504-3 (sc)
ISBN: 978-1-4669-4503-6 (e)

Trafford rev. 1/23/2013

 www.trafford.com

North America & international
toll-free: 1 888 232 4444 (USA & Canada)
phone: 250 383 6864 • fax: 812 355 4082

TABLE OF CONTENTS

CHAPTER I

Historical Background of Aquaculture:

Aquaculture has been in existence for hundreds and thousands of years in some countries, but in others has been introduced only in recent years. In different countries, aquaculture has different historical backgrounds.

Definition:

The term aquaculture means aquatic farming including aquatic animals and plants in fresh, brackish and marine environments. Pond culture, raceways, cage, pen and raft cultures are part of it. Species including fish, oysters, mussels, sea weeds are grown. In brief, aquaculture means aquatic farming of various categories and species including fish farming. Fish farming, per se, is not aquaculture, but aquaculture includes fish farming (Pillay, 1993).

In Asia:

In China and the Indo-Pacific regions, fish culture is very old. The origin of fish culture in China is said to have started during Wen Fang administration. The last ruler of Shang Dynasty had Wen Fang confined to an estate in Honan province in 1135-1122 B.C. It was at this time that Wen Fang built some ponds. He planted fingerlings in these ponds and studied their growth and movements. In 460 B.C., Fan Li wrote his "Fish Culture Classic," which described in great detail the results of the many experiments made by Fan Li and

others. At this time the culturing of carp for pleasure changed to rearing of carp for food.
The size of the ponds expanded and the ventures became more profitable (Brown, 1983).

The later writings of Chow Mit of the Sung Dynasty described in some details the
collection of carp fry from rivers and methods of rearing them in ponds (Pillay, 1983). The
earliest type of fish to have been cultivated was the common carp (*Cyprinus carpio*). It was
first cultured in China. It was then introduced in several other countries of Asia and the Far
East.

In Asia and the Far East, especially in China, fish is regarded as the best kind of food,
highly valued by every family. If a person wanted to please someone, he gave him fish to
eat. Fish in China was served, and still is served, at all festivals, social functions, family
celebrations and religious gatherings (Ling, 1977). The habit of keeping fish in ponds in rural
China started with Chinese fishermen who kept their surplus fish alive temporarily before
using them (Ling, 1977). These ponds were first formed by damming one side of a river bed.
The fishermen realized that if the walls of the dam were strong and the fish therein supplied
with food, then captured animals can grow in there providing the family with a constant food
supply. At some other times when the water levels of rivers and streams rose, people would
build trapping ponds on the banks of the rivers. Many different sizes and kinds of fish were
trapped in these ponds. These trapping ponds, as time went, developed into fish culture
operations (Ling, 1977).

As stated earlier, common carp was the first type of fish that was cultivated in China,
but in the 6th century, this common carp lost significance in China. This was because of
identifying the common carp, as Lee, which was also the family name of the emperor of

China. The name Lee was sacred; the idea of culturing lee in ponds and catching and eating it was completely forbidden. The Chinese carp was then replaced by four additional species, namely grass carp, silver carp, bighead carp and mud carp (Ling, 1977).

The traditional systems of aquaculture were practiced by common rural farmers without help from the government. But at the beginning of the 20th century, the government felt that new ideas and concepts should be applied to fish farming. Modern science had already been introduced in the country. Young men and scholars were sent abroad to study biology; thus some of these young scholars became fisheries biologists and fisheries culturists.

In Japan and Surrounding Nations:

Fish farming has been going on for thousands of years, but commercial fish farming started about 150 years ago. It was in the 1930's that the government of Japan placed emphasis on marine harvest. During the second world war, fresh water fish farming expanded. In 1950, the output of shallow sea cultured fish reached 48,000 MT. This included mussels, mollusks, and seaweeds which expanded from 48,000 MT to 917,000 MT. The fresh water cultured fish production increased from 5,000 MT in 1950 to 90,000 MT in 1978.

In Japan there are six major species of freshwater fish produced in ponds or running water, enclosures. Fish ponds in Japan are categorized into: (1) agricultural ponds, mainly for agriculture and where the water level may vary considerably; (2) specially built ponds of concrete, with running water; (3) still water ponds used primarily for culturing and with constant water levels; and (4) running water enclosures. In a few cases, pens, cages, and nets are used. The six major species grown in the country include rainbow trout, Japanese eel, common carp, ayn or sweetfish, and lastly tilapia (Brown, 1983).

Indonesia, the Philippines and Taiwan are the world's leaders in milkfish farming. This system of farming was first started 500 years ago. It was then introduced in Philippines and Taiwan in the 16th century. In Taiwan, milkfish farming was already practiced during the administration of Cheng Cheng-Kung. Today, over five billion fry are needed for the three major milkfish culturing countries of Indonesia, Philippines and Taiwan. This provides employment to many unskilled workers in these three countries (Ling, 1977).

In Southeast Asia, rivers everywhere are filled with fish. The people of these nations practice fish farming so that they might have fish available whenever they want them (Ling, 1977). There are many varieties of religions in these nations which prohibit the eating of pork and chicken, but everywhere people are allowed to eat fish. People in these nations love eating fish and thus fish farming development is greater in Southeast Asia than it is elsewhere in the world (Kigeya, 1995).

Thais are known for their shrimp farming. Burma is famous for many Indian and Chinese carps. Cambodia is known for fish from the inland freshwater lakes and part of the Mekong River system. Mekong produces 40% of the fish consumed in Cambodia. *Carps* are produced in North and South Vietnam. Fish farming in the regions stated above has been hindered by political and military unrest (Kigeya, 1995). Malaysia is very famous for the rice field fish culture. Singapore is important for shrimp pond production. Indonesia, mainly in Java, is known for milkfish culture in pens, canals and lagoons.

As stated earlier, Taiwan is significant for milkfish farming. They have small sized ponds with excellent managerial skills. Taiwan is also known for their oyster farming and well developed polyculture systems. This includes the polyculture of fish integrated with ducks and other agricultural and animal husbandry undertakings. Taiwan also produces *shrimp* either in monoculture ponds or integrated with milkfish in ponds. Eel culture has been developed in less than 20 years (Ling, 1977).

Hong Kong is an international trading center for fingerlings. Polyculture of Chinese fish with *mullet* is practiced on large scale. In Hong Kong, most fish are sent to markets alive. As already mentioned, fish farming has a long history in Asia and almost every nation has tried to grow many varieties of species such as *crustaceans, mollusks,* and *seaweeds.* There are many species cultivated in Southeast Asian nations, but not all could be discussed here in these few brief lines.

Europe:

According to Edminster (1947), fish farming spread throughout Europe during the Middle Ages. Fish culturing was mainly promoted and recorded by religious groups. Important chiefs and kings conducted fish culture in their private back yard fish ponds. In the 18th century, Charlemagne was described as keeping his ponds in good repair. The techniques in these old days were in handling the spawn, feeding fish, arranging and fertilizing the ponds.

In 1420, a monk by the name of Dom Pinchon conducted artificial fecundating of trout eggs by pressing out spawn and milt from female and male fish. These were mixed to gather in water and as a result eggs were fertilized under man's control. This was the beginning of science of pisciculture or breeding of fish.

Pond fish farming spread to England in the 16th century. In 1514, *carp* was introduced in Britain and *pike* was started in 1537. North recognized the balancing of fish in ponds. He was the first person to mention the correct amount of fish to be stocked in a pond. He suggested 300 *carps* per acre. He also mentioned the possibility of using carnivorous species of fish to balance the stock in ponds. *Perches* could be used as they devour their own species more than they devour other species. He warned against using *pikes* as he said that they would devour the best fish. But Boccius recommended that *jack* or pikes could be used to cut down prolific production of *carps*. North also mentioned the use of fertilizers in ponds. Most fertilizers were organic such as sheep manure, malt, grains, carrion, and slaughter-house refuse. As fish farming techniques improved, the knowledge of fish culture spread throughout various nations of Europe. In some countries, fish farming started early and in some, took time to catch up.

Italy:

Italy is known for *trout* and this culture originated in mountains called Trentino at the beginning of the 20th century. There was a common belief that since natural *trouts* are found in mountain brooks, their trout farms should be constructed in the mountains. These early fish farmers believed that altitude was important for fish culture. They did not know, however, that limiting factor was high quantity of water with constant flow and constant temperatures. For many years, trout farming was done in mountain areas where water was scarce, winters were long, and land was restricted. Thus trout produced in mountains regions were slow to grow. It took 24 months to mature and as a result there wasn't enough to supply the Italian people. Until 1965, Italy was a good market for other European nations' productions like Denmark (Brown, 1983).

But around about 1960 some Italian farmers discovered that *trout* could be produced in plains south of the Alps. In parts of this area were large marshes fed by springs. The temperatures at the springs were 12° to 13°C or 54° to 55°F. In 1965 or 1966, Italy changed from an importing nation to a trout exporting nation. In 1979 production had reached 19,900 MT. Trout exports increased even more dramatically from 1000 MT to 3819 MT which was 282%. This was an outstanding achievement for Italy.

Italy started exporting trout fish to France (60%), Germany (25%) and other European nations (15%) (Brown, 1983). Other nations of Europe such as Belgium, Switzerland, Austria, Denmark and others started importing great amounts of fish from Italy.

Salvador farms are probably the largest fish farms in the world. They are situated on the Northeastern side near Treviso. These farms are under one private individual. They produced several thousands of metric tons of fish. They also produce eyed eggs. At these Salvador farms, spawning fish are raised, eggs are hatched, fish are grown out to market size, but all of them in one farm facility.

Another rainbow trout farm is at Milan and produces about 1000 MT of fish annually. The farm is supplied by several springs. The farm has earthen and concrete raceways. The farm brings in eyed-eggs from Alps, hatches the eggs and grows the fish up to a marketable size. Sales are made in Italy, France, and Germany.

Species cultivated in Italy include *rainbow trout, eel, catfish* and other brackish water

species.

France:

France also is famous for *rainbow trout*. Trout culture in this country is undergoing

changes. In 1974, production reached 15,000 MT and in 1979 reached 18,000 MT.

In 1975 there were 700 trout farmers in France. Two hundred of these farmers buy

fish which weight 160 grams each and keep them in their ponds and increase their weight to

about 180-200 grams. These fish are then resold at higher prices. Such people are not

necessarily fish farmers but rather fish traders. The other 500 fish farmers are smaller

producers. They produce between 10 to 20 MT per year. It is estimated that 50 large

farmers account to about one-half of total production.

France as a country is divided into seven fish farming regions such as North, East,

Parisian Basin, Normandy, Brittany, Southwest Central, Southeast, and Pyrenees. In 1972

Brittany was the largest trout producer region in the whole of France. It produced 26.4% of

total production, the North produced 16.7%, Normandy 14.7%, Southeast 12.4%, and

Pyrenees 11.1% (Brown, 1983).

The northern half of France represents 70% of trout production and the Southern half

produces only 30%. Every fish producer has his or her own markets. The northern half,

including Brittany, Normandy, North, East and Parisian Basin regions, exchange their fish

among themselves. Someone from Brittany could sell his fish in the North or East or

wherever he could find markets. The northern part of France produces two-thirds of the fish using only one-third of the producers. The southern section of France produces slightly more than one-third of the fish using about two-thirds of the farmers.

France has always been importing more *rainbow trout* than they exported. In 1960, France imported 1905 MT, but exported only 158 MT. In 1968 imports and exports increased. In 1973 and 1974, France exported most of the *rainbow trout* to Belgium and this accounted for 89% of the total exports. Whereas, most of the farmers believe that most of their fish exports go to West Germany.

Some farmers are small producers using sometimes one or two hired people. The fish farm produces the fish eggs, fingerlings and fry. They have disease free spawnings stock. They have no problem of pollution at all on their farms.

Fish farmers in France have a problem of feed costs. The lowest truck lots would cost $333 per MT to a high of $378 per MT for 50% protein feeds for young fry.

Although most of the farmers do not have pollution on their farms, they also run risks when they import fish from other countries. These fish introduce virus diseases such as viral hemorrhagic septicemia, and infectious pancreatic necrosis as well as bacterial diseases like carp yersiniosis. To eliminate the spread of diseases in France, the government has instituted methods of helping fish farmers to rid themselves of diseases that might have been introduced from outside France and also stiffer regulations have been instituted to check on species of fish that come into France. Salmonid farms in the country are monitored to eliminate any chance of disease.

France has problems of markets for their fish products. There is high competition between France and other fish producing countries such as Chile, Japan, and many other European fish producing nations like Italy, Switzerland and Belgium.

Species such as *rainbow trout, brown trout, carp, European eels* are some of the types of fish that are cultured in France.

Sweden:

Noble crayfish have been cultured in Sweden for a very long time. *Crayfish* were popular in the 16th Century in Sweden. They were planted in various locations in the country. Great quantities were fished for several centuries in the southern and central parts of Sweden. At the turn of this century about 1000 to 1500 tons were caught, but today only a tenth of that is being caught. The government has tried to stock some of these waters with crayfish so that fish could be increased, but the diseases which destroyed the first stock still come back to destroy the implanted stock.

In Sweden, crayfish farming could be extensive or semi-extensive or intensive. The intensive is usually indoor and is still undergoing development. It requires great numbers of crayfish to be kept in the farm for it to yield profits. Profits can be made if one aims at raising fry for sale (OCDE, 1989).

The best method of culturing crayfish is by using semi-extensive farming in excavated ponds. *Crayfish* need hiding places for protection. When they shed their shells they become attractive as prey for other crayfish. Hiding places can be built with stones, roof tiles, and perforated bricks. A pipe of 5-6 cm diameter can also act as a good hiding place. It should be tied off at one end.

Feeding crayfish is not difficult, because natural plants and insects in the water are sufficient for food. When other types of food are found to be needed, half-boiled root vegetables like potatoes and carrots are used. These should not be left at the bottom of the pond as they will rot and cause oxygen deficiency.

In Sweden, two methods of designing crayfish farms are available. One way is to look for a long possible shore length. Another way is to get an island in the water. The hiding places should be built of stones or bricks. There should be continuous supply of running water, so that the farm does not freeze in winter or dry out in summer. Agriculture pesticides are particularly dangerous to crayfish.

Fast moving water through a farm should be watched as it can cause stress to crayfish. Fish should not be allowed to enter the farm as they are potential predators. All inlets and outlets should be closed with nets to prevent any incoming fish (OCDE, 1989).

Crayfish can be planted as adults or as fry. With adults one male for every three females should be set out. Fry should be placed at a depth of 0.5 to 1.5 meters. They should be put at a density of 10 per meter offshore. In addition to the crayfish, the rainbow trout and the Atlantic salmons are also cultured here in Sweden. Apart from those three species above, there are others such as sea trout, brown trout, brook trout, lake trout, and Arctic char. Only *rainbow trout* and *Atlantic trout* are the only two species cultured for food consumption (OCDE, 1989).

There are about 100 private fish farms raising fish for the domestic food. The farms are small, about .5-50 MT annually and averaging about 4.0 MT of production. Sweden imports fish like in 1974, 550 MT were imported from Denmark. Less than 100 MT of *rainbow trout* were imported from Norway, and 100-150 MT of *fresh iced salmon* were imported from Norway (Brown, 1983).

Nearly all cultured fish in the country come from the Southern part of Sweden; where water is warmest and conducive to fish farming activities. Production of *trout* and *salmon* are expected to increase as research findings on culturing these two species are adopted. The government is putting more efforts in restocking. The government is restocking *brown trout*, *lake trout*, and *Arctic char* (Brown, 1983).

Switzerland:

There are two types of species cultured in Switzerland for food. These are *rainbow trout* and *brown trout*. Total production of both in 1974 was 300 MT. All fish production is used locally. It amounts to about 23% of total domestic fish requirements. Switzerland imports fish from other European nations.

For fish produced in the country, *rainbow trout* spawns in February and March while *brown trout* spawns in November, December and January. After spawning, fry are kept in special concrete tanks for some time until they are six centimeters. After that they are placed in grow out facilities. These are earthen ponds. It takes about 12-24 months to raise *rainbow trout* and *brown trout* to a size where they can be sold in markets. Usually fish are sold when they weigh about 180 and 200 grams. All domestic cultured fish are sold alive. Eighty

percent of imported *trout* are purchased alive.

Carp are also produced in Switzerland for food. These are limited because of

inappropriate water temperatures, which result into slow growth and limited demand (Brown,

1983). The government of Switzerland also produces young fry, fingerlings, and year-old

fish. The species produced most are *northern pike, brown trout, lake white fish, stealhead

trout, lake trout,* and *grayling.*

United Kingdom:

Although United Kingdom is one of the nations of Europe where fish farming has

been done for centuries, yet much of the progress had taken place in the last three decades.

The United Kingdom ranks sixth among fish farming nations in Europe. Like all other

European nations, the majority of domestic fish production is concentrated on *rainbow trout,*

but due to media commercialization, other species such as *salmon, Dover sole, turbot, eels,

crayfish* and *carp* are getting attention.

The government has research laboratories working with the industry to overcome the

biological problems, diseases, marketing, and other related issues.

In specialized areas, individual farmers are forming associations such as the Mollusks

and Crustacea Farmers Association, Shellfish Association, and Trout Farmers Association.

In 1978, rainbow trout farmers were about 160 in the United Kingdom. One-third of

these farmers were in Scotland and most of the farmers are small scale and they sell their fish

at the farm gate, local hotels and restaurants. The trout producers have been forced to organize so as to produce better quality products of fish which have size, weight which the supermarkets, and large buyers require (Brown, 1983).

There are three major problems in rainbow trout farming. (1) Disease has been and is still a big problem in the industry. Despite the fact that the government is trying all it can to prevent diseases in the country, some very large farms such as one multinational industry had to close down due to the spread of infectious pancreative necrosis. (2) Rating is a problem on buildings and other installations. Many times fish farmers are rated in the same way as industrialists. This results into unfair taxation which sometimes makes these businesses end in failures. (3) Lack of cooperation in marketing, mainly among small scale farmers, results in many different quality standards, erratic supply, and no dynamic advertising to educate the consumers. Many family members have never eaten trout or they might have eaten it once or twice in a restaurant. Such people need to be educated to make greater use of fish in their diet.

Salmon in the United Kingdom are cultured in cages and through difficult operations, many companies such as Fitch Lovell, Booker McConnell, etc., are making profits (Brown, 1983).

Salmon production are confined to Scotland. Sites for such operation have risen from one to forty-seven in 1980. These sites include those in fresh and salt waters. The total tonnage was 538 MT in 1980.

Red tides have caused heavy losses of *salmon* in certain areas and now special groups are studying these issues to look for solution. Good, suitable sites are becoming scarce as cage farming requires good and unpolluted water. These sites should be away from commercial leisure traffic with some protection from elements in form of hills or other barriers preventing ravages to the farm.

Eels were confined to collection of *elvers* for exports to other countries like Holland. These *eels* are collected from two areas in the United Kingdom: (1) Seven estuary and (2) Loch Neagh in Northern Ireland. Because of large profits which are involved in these businesses, large companies are now taking part in growing *elvers* using heated power plants effluent. This type of farming is likely to be the most progressive of all fish farming in the United Kingdom (Brown, 1983).

The growing of *crayfish* at the moment is confined to individuals and farmers who are experimenting with low level production. The potential for the export to nearby market in France is great. Marketing will be difficult unless large quantities of crayfish are available. The present production is a little more than 100 MT per year; and all are for export. At least four or five carp farms have emerged in the last few years. The growing season is confined to five months of the year. The market is still confined to the United Kingdom. One of the farms produces *mirror carps* and *Crucian carp* for stocking in lakes and commercial ponds. There are other species such as ornamental fish that exist in the country, like *koi, carp, tench,* and *orfe,* etc.

Poland:

In Poland, 305,000 ha are represented by lakes, 104,000 by rivers and dams, 60,000 ha by ponds. The most important producer of fish in Poland are state fish farms and the Polish Anglers Association. The state fish farm use 91% of the total lake area, 86% of the pond area. The Polish Anglers Association use about 70% of total area of rivers and dam

reservoirs; and 6% of total lake area. Polish anglers have the right to carry out sport fishing,

on the majority of lakes which are managed by state fish farms.

There are a few tiny spots in Poland such as small lakes, ponds, pools, old riverbeds,

quarry lakes which are not mentioned anywhere in literature and yet they are important for

fishery values, especially for recreations.

Common carp is the most important species cultured in ponds. This constitutes 100%

of total fish production. *Common carp* production in Poland is on the increase. Although

there are lots of problems in carp culture, yet the production is increasing. The reason for

this increase is the improved biotechnique. The pond carp culture is carried out by the state

pond farms which were started after World War II.

Ponds in Poland have values such as: (1) value of ponds as an element of complex

management of water resource; (2) value of ponds as an element of local management of

water resource; (3) value of ponds an element of protection, preservation and shaping of the

natural environment; (4) value of ponds as an element of various other nonproduction

benefits; and (5) value of ponds as an element of local economic activation (Brown, 1983).

Despite the fact that there are problems in fish farming in Poland, its general development is

good. In 1977, the average production of *carp* was 900 kg/ha. Many farms in the same year

obtained yields of 2000 kg/ha. In Poland the policy of the government was to utilize as much

of the natural food resources of ponds.

There is a general increase of commercial lake fish catches. This is mainly due to the

increase of bream and roach and in the increase of fish artificially stocked. But the yield in the other species is decreasing. The increase in lake fish production is a result of good management skills used. If the proper management of lakes is missing, lake fish catch will go down. Recreation activity in fishing on lakes has had impact. This does not have an effect on lake fish stocking (Bennett, 1971).

Lake fish production in Poland is slightly lower than pond fish production. Although pond fish culture is doing better than lake fish production, it is less economic. Lake fish farming in Poland has two basic forms of cage culture: (1) cage culture in which fish are artificially fed, and (2) cage fish culture in which fish are not fed but keeps on floating on lakes and feeds naturally.

In the same way, more intensive forms of *trout* culture which are independent of natural food resources are not much promoted; due to their significant protein requirements.

About 1000 MT of fish are caught annually in rivers and dam reservoirs by fishery cooperatives. Apart from this, the rest of the river catches are taken by individual anglers in the form of recreational catches from rivers and dam reservoirs. There are other species that are cultured in Poland such as cage culture carried out in rivers, heated affluent and inshore marine waters (Brown, 1980).

Hungary:

Hungary is a landlocked nation in central Europe. Because it is landlocked, the population is accustomed to the fresh water fish which are available through domestic production. The majority of the indigenous fish in Hungary belong to the families *Cyprinidae* and *Percidae* which are warm water fish. The fishing rights belong to the state on all natural waters of the country, about 130,000 ha. The state then grants these rights on conditions,

such as organizations which are considered suitable to utilize these water areas. These

organizations should be the following: state farms, agricultural cooperatives, fishery

cooperatives, research institutes, and the Hungarian National Angling Union.

The production of common carp is the most important. The climate and the

topography of the country are particularly suitable for the growing of pond fish. The total

pond area in operation is about 20,000 ha (Bennett, 1971). Other supplementary fish species

together with *carp* are practiced. This includes the predatory fish, like *pike-perch*. The

introduction of *Chinese carp* led to important changes in Hungarian fish farming (Brown,

1983). The acclimatization program started with species such as *grass carp, bighead*, and the

silver carp. All these are herbivorous fish species. The main object was to increase yield

without changing the methods of feeding.

A survey which was conducted in 1973-1978 which involved 60% of the pond farms

and 80% of the pond areas of the country indicated that three herbivorous species are used in

production by pond farms.

Pond farmers stock their farms with *carp* and herbivorous species in various amounts.

These amounts are dictated by market requirements and the natural conditions. A complete

production cycle can be found on larger farms where specialization is possible. About 30%

of hatching is concentrated in the warm water hatchery at Szazhalombatta (Edminster, 1947).

Trout farming has just been introduced in Hungary. It was in 1976 that two minor

trout farms are operated in the country. Their main task was to supply food fish for the

domestic market and partly to provide stocking material for the natural water areas. One large trout farm was raised in 1976 and the main species raised here is rainbow trout. Smaller quantities of brown trout are also produced as stocking material for sport fishing waters (Brown, 1983).

In Hungary, there is a program concerned with large river draining operations. These operations have greatly affected fishery activities in the country. The drainage of large food areas has lead to reduction of fish breeding areas. As a result, there is reduction in river fish stock. This massive reduction in fish production can be counteracted by massive backwater fish production; and sport fishing activity. Fishery cooperatives operating in the backwater have recognized the possibility of massive fish production this way.

Apart from backwater fish production, there is fish production in cages. This is done only on experimental basis in the country. The prices of fish feeds, which are too high, make fish production in cages very uneconomical.

The marketing possibilities that exist in Hungary plays a big role in the economics of fish farming. Stocking materials are mostly marketed through direct deliveries between fish farms and the companies concerned on basis of contracts concluded many years in advance. The market is less affected by exports because exports were limited by the state during the time Hungary was communist, but now the trend is slightly different although not that much different.

United States of America:

In 1792, Charles Carroll, a signer of the Declaration of Independence, had a diary which constituted a journal on the management of his estate at Doughreghan Manor in Howard County, Maryland (Edminster, 1947).

The interest of fish farming in the United States came from England. But in America, there were many local natural streams, ponds and lakes that the need for artificial fish ponds did not attract attention. Since there was no pressing reasons for these ponds, little was done until late in the 19th century.

In the 1850's, there was an occurrence in which *black bass* were transplanted from their native water to new areas where they had not lived before. This technique began in New England and spread to many other states. In 1854, *black bass* species were carried from Ohio River to Potomac. At that time the whole river was stocked. This resulted into great numbers of *chubs, minnows, suckers,* but after some years now, *black bass* is scarce on the Potomac River. This is expected because one of the herbivorous types of fish became scarce, then *black bass* began eating each other. As years progressed, the European system of carp culture was to be brought here from abroad. As fishing in streams and rivers waned, carp ponds were advocated for farmers, and a wave of interest swept over the country. The enthusiasm for growing *carp* soon declined. The ponds were left uncared for and *carps* escaped into our rivers and lakes. Thus, these *carps* were scattered all over for their bad effects on aquatic vegetation and native fish (Edminister, 1947).

It was well over in this century that interest in fish farming started again. The person who was responsible for the rise of fish pond interest was Professor George C. Embody of

Cornell University, the late fish culturist. It was in 1915 that he published In The Fishpond in the Cornell Reading Courses series. Embody's bulletin dealt with advanced thinking about fish ponds at that time and revealed points of progress over the earlier customs.. He relied on native species for stocking the ponds. He encouraged farmers to take interest in *black basses, sunfishes, perch, rock bass, bullheads, calico bass,* and the like. These were termed edible fish, that their food was largely vegetable (Edminster, 1947).

Rainbow trout is the only specie of cold fresh water that is cultured commercially in the United States. It is cultured in 48 states out of the fifty-one states. Texas, Louisiana and Mississippi do not grow the *rainbow trout.* Since 1975, some *trout* have been cultured in catfish ponds in Mississippi but on experimental basis. In 1979, there were 653 growers of all types (Anon, 1979). The leading states are Idaho, Wisconsin, Colorado, Michigan and Pennsylvania. In addition to this, there are 1086 operators of *trout* fee-fish-out ponds. In 1979, there were 200 in Colorado and 197 in Pennsylvania alone.

The business of raising *trout* began in the 1870s. It was after 1900 that *rainbow trout* was introduced into commercial fish farming.

Today it is safe to say that *rainbow trout* is developing very well. Feed manufacturers state that they are selling more trout feed than ever before. Similar statements are made by egg producers. This increased fee-fish-out ponds. Production of processed trout is also increasing. According to Anon (1980), nine states including Idaho, California, Georgia, Missouri, Pennsylvania, Washington, Wisconsin, Alabama and Arkansas indicated to have produced 42,576,000 trout which weighed 12,800,000 kg.

Egg Incubation:

After spawning, eggs are acclimated to the water temperature at the hatchery. Eggs are hatched ten months out of the year. Only in July and August, eggs are not available.

Fry:

The emergent york-sac fry are removed from incubator trays or baskets and put into troughs. Then they are fed on hand feeding and automatic feeding procedures. Of the 41,180,000 fry hatched in 1973, 6,590,000 million died from different causes.

Fingerlings:

At this stage, fish are outside and they grow sometimes over 2.5 cm per month. They are fed 4-5% of their body weight. At some farms they are separated by size groups and they are distributed to new ponds.

Stocker:

At this stage, fish are sent to farm pond operations or fee-fishing establishments. They remain there until they are processable size. At this time, the growth rate has slowed down and food amounts also change. The fish are fed 1-3% of body weight per day.

Marketables:

Fish are marketable at 30 cm long. They are shipped from rearing ponds to processing plants and in 1973, 26,910,000 fish were sold live or processed. Thus survivability after hatching was 65% (Brown, 1983). Private warm water fish culture in United States began in 1920s and early 1930s. During this time, a few individuals began raising *minnows* to supply the growing demand for fish bait for sport fishing. After World War II, with the boom in farm ponds and reservoir construction the demand for *minnows* increased. By 1940, a dozen or more private operators were producing fish bait (Edminster, 1947).

In 1961, fish farming industry was again expanding. This time it was based on more experience and early results of research in respect to catfish which have proved to be the most desirable and profitable warm water specie. In 1963, about 6830 ha were devoted to warm water fish culture, and 960 ha for catfish.

Harvesting:

In harvesting catfish from a tank or cage is done by lifting the fish with a dip net and loaded into transfer container and placed in the live haul for transportation. Race ways are 6 m wide and can be harvested using seine about twice this width. The seine is dragged the length of the race way segment, crowding the fish together and then they will be dipped out. Another alternative is to drain the segment. The net is set at the headwall, fish will be trapped as they leave the race way.

Ponds harvesting are much more complex. United States has some of the largest ponds in the world. Some of them can be as large as a small lake. The water will be too much to be drained. This harvesting will require a few days of preparation. The best method to be used will be to drain the pond using pumps or ditches which are prepared in advance. Many fish are bound to die due to lack of oxygen (Brown, 1983).

Usually the fish in such large ponds will exceed what the market can absorb. Some smaller ponds of less than 16 ha, haul seines can be used to harvest them. Mechanical haul seine can be used.

These mechanized wire-cable puller, winds the cable. As the fish are gathered in a harvesting area, they are dipped out by a dip net. The most recent technique to be used involves a live car. As fish are crowded, they swim into the live car. When a live car is filled, is detached and another car is attached. The filled live car is floated into the deeper water to remove the fish from muddy water.

When all the live cars are filled they are lined against the bank from where a mechanized brailer will be used to dip the fish out onto a sorting table in the water. The smaller fish of less than 350 g are released back into the water. Those larger than 350 g are loaded to the waiting truck to be transported to the processing plants.

When such large ponds are harvested, some fish are taken to processing plants, some are sold to live haulers who in turn sell them to the producers for food production. Some are sold to fee-fish-out operators for stocking farm ponds and some are sold to fish-out recreation ponds and others to farm stock ponds (Brown, 1980).

There are considerable imports from other countries also. In 1969, there were 1,710,000 kg of dressed catfish imported. Since that time, catfish imports have increased considerably.

Crayfish are found on every continent except Africa and Antarctica. There are about 500 species everywhere in the world. But 250 species are found in North America (Brown, 1983). *Crayfish* begin their lives in a burrow or a hole on the wall of a pond or a lake wall.

The female hides in a burrow and in May or June, the male deposits sperms. When the female lays eggs, they are fertilized by the sperms deposited by male *crayfish*. The fertilized eggs are attached to female's body using slimy sticky subsistence. Some *crayfish* may have as few as 10 eggs but others may lay as many as 700 eggs. *Crayfish* are caught everywhere in North America. In Oregon, *crayfish* are produced in abundance. In Washington state, crayfishing is done considerably. Most of *crayfish* farming is done in Louisiana and more than 4,500,000 kg are produced in Louisiana annually. *Crayfish* currently are farmed in rice-field ponds, wooded ponds, and open ponds. In rice-field ponds, *crayfish* are rotated with the rotation of rice fields.

Wooded ponds make poor *crayfish* ponds. Dense growths of trees and shrubs hinder harvesting. Usually these wooded ponds have problems of oxygen depletion. The water in such ponds is usually acidic. This results in a low pH and a low total hardness. Although wooded areas are poor for fish production, yet wooded environments are usually utilized for *crayfish* farming. These wooded areas are usually good for nothing. Fish farming could be the better alternative, as these areas would be unused, so a little bit of fish is better than nothing.

Open ponds are used for crayfish farming. The procedure for farming in open ponds is the same as for wooded or for rice-fields.

The future of *crayfish* culture is very bright. The ponds devoted to *crayfish* farming are increasing rapidly. In Louisiana, over 4850 ha were devoted to *crayfish* culture in 1969. In 1979, the area had increased to 16,2000 ha (Anon, 1979A).

Processing:

In the processing plant, *crayfish* are stored in a cooler and at 3%. The following day, the live *crayfish* are removed from the cooler and they are then washed and thoroughly cleaned. The clean *crayfish* are placed in stainless steel tanks for blanching. The *crayfish* are blanched for 5 minutes and no spices are added. The blanching does three things: (1) kills the crayfish; (2) destroys or inhibits bacteria and enzymes in crayfish; and (3) facilitates manual peeling. The blanched crayfish are transported to the processing room where the meat is separated from the shell manually. More than 50 persons are employed for this job.

Marine Culture:

Salmons are cultured in three states in the United States. These are Washington and Oregon on the West Coast and Maine on the East Coast. In 1980, there were two farms specializing in fingerlings production, three farms specializing in fingerlings and pan-sized cultured *salmons* and three farms produced only pan-sized *salmons*. Two of these eight farms were engaged in sea ranching.

Salmon production in Washington and Oregon has had many difficulties. The initial culturing was started by the Bureau of Commercial Fisheries in 1967 in floating net-pens. In Washington, private growers are not allowed to spawn fish. Eye-eggs are bought from public agencies. In Oregon, private spawning of *chum salmon* was permitted in 1971. In 1973, *Coho* and *Chinook salmon* were also added. In Washington, Oregon and Maine, only smaller amounts of *Chinook* and *Chum salmon* are cultured. Interests are centered on *Coho* because of its resistance to disease and willingness to accept dry feed (Brown, 1983).

Sea ranching is another culturing technique, but instead of feeding the fish throughout the production, smolts are released in the sea. The mature fish return after 2 to 5 years to the point of release and rearing. Sea ranching is legal only in Oregon, an extension of public restocking efforts which have been in existence for years (Brown, 1983).

Shrimp:

There is only one commercial marine shrimp culturing farm in the United States and it is the Maxifarms, Inc., Panama City, Florida. The experimental production was started in 1968. Farming is extensive compared to the Intensive in Japan. The farm has 1012 ha of water and 121 ha of marine lakes with pumped water exchanges from an upland leased from a private individual. The bottom of the farm contains benthic organisms abound. It was the goal of the farm management that the *shrimp* feed on these organisms. This reduces the cost of feeding these animals on the farm.

Manifarms has made it possible to grow two consecutive crops of *shrimp* in the very same areas. The first crop is the *brown shrimp*. These are hatched in February and March, but were planted in April and May. They are moved through the nursery into the grow out areas and harvested in June and August. The hatchery then moves to *white shrimp*. These are hatched in May and June period. These move through the same areas arriving in the grow-out areas after the summer harvest of the *brown shrimp*. The third crop of *pink shrimp*, cannot be carried out because of the winter. It is difficult to hold juvenile *shrimp* in cold months. This can only happen if the growing area is deep, so that the cold does not penetrate

through and comparing the efforts and the difficulties one has to go through, third cropping is
not worth it.

Harvesting:

Harvesting *shrimp* at sea, the catch is done manually. Sometime as little as 10% of
what is caught is shrimp. The other trash fish and other materials are sorted out by hand and
thrown overboard. While trawling continues, the crew squeeze their heads off the shrimp by
hand. Then the tails are placed in wire baskets, and after washing, finally store these with
ice below the deck. Washing *shrimp* on the boat is necessary to prevent spotting by
polyphenoloxidase enzymes. When a load is accumulated, the trawler returns to port to
unload and stock up on provisions and then returns to fishing at sea. Ships sometimes stay
at sea for a week or more at times.

Manifarms use similar trawlers, but the farmed waters contain nothing or probably
little, but mostly *shrimp*, there is no need to sort them by hand on deck. The catch is dropped
on deck, spread out and layered with ice. During the time the crew spends at sea, the *shrimp*
are covered with a canvas. After hours of trawling, the boat will have several thousand
pounds on its deck. It returns to the shore on the farm where the catch is unloaded with a
vacuum lift with the aid of a heavy stream of water (Brown, 1980).

When shrimping goes on the sea, the *shrimp* are emptied on to a transfer net on a
special skiff used for the trawling. Every hour or so, the skiff stops at a docking point so that
the transfer net can be lifted; and be emptied into a tank of ice water mounted on a trailer.
Every few hours this is pulled to a vacuum lift for final unloading.

The *shrimp* are removed from the skiff into a big tank of ice water from which they are transformed by a metal chainlink type of conveyor belt. The *shrimp* on the conveyor pass across an inspection table where debris and the relatively few fish, *crabs*, etc. are removed by hand. The *shrimp* are delivered untouched by a human hand. This minimizes the bacterial count (Brown, 1983). All states in America, except Delaware and Mississippi operated at least one state hatcher during 1973 (Anon, 1974). The total number of state fish hatchery was 425 of which 297 produced cold water fish, 73 produced warm water fish, 29 produced walleye and northern pike and 26 produced various combinations of fish.

In the United States, Washington state had the largest amounts of hatcheries with 66, 57 of which produced *anodromous Salmonoids*. Oregon had 31 hatcheries and produced mainly *Pacific Salmon* and *Steelhead*. The number of nationwide system of state hatcheries is rising. There were 91 national hatcheries in 39 states operated by the United States Fish and Wildlife Service in 1978. Some of these reared *trout* and others reared *trout* and other different types of fish. But only a few national hatcheries raised warm water fish only. But about a third produced them with some other types of fish (Brown, 1983).

Canada:

Aquaculture in Canada started in 1857 in the province of Quebec. *Atlantic Salmon* and speckled trout were the fist species that were cultured in Canada. The Newcastle Hatchery in Ontario was established in 1866. It influenced both private and governmental aquacultural developments in the country. The construction of major hatcheries along the Great Lakes which began in 1975 influenced the culture method which was taken up by North

America, when they started culturing *coregonid, percoid* and *esocid* and other types of fish. By the British North American Act of 1867, the overall responsibility for the Canadian freshwater and marine fisheries lies with the federal government.

In 1972, there were some 21 federal and 31 provincial government hatcheries, 163 commercial hatcheries and an additional 113 licensed domestic operations. Both the provincial and federal government have followed traditional approach in carrying out artificial propagation of fish both in terms of species cultured and other aspects of hatcheries. Commercial fish farmers in the same year 1972, excluding experimental harvests of stocked *rainbow trout*, marketed almost 13 million fish weighing an estimated 485 MT. This was mainly *rainbow* and *speckled trout* (Brown, 1980).

The commercial farming of freshwater *salmonoids* for human consumption in Canada is of recent origin. This was so because there was local respect for the *speckled trout* as a sport fish; and because people did not understand whether Atlantic and Pacific *Salmons* could be profitably cultured to a marketable size. Thus, the government was hesitant to change legislation which prohibited sales of prized sport fish to accommodate a new aspect of private commercial enterprise.

In 1972, food sales of Canadian products totaled to 1.1 million fish which weighed about 352,227 kg and this was mainly *rainbow trout*. *Speckled trout* for human consumption are still prohibited by law in Quebec. Despite restrictions by federal and provincial governments on the importation and transfer of eggs and fish, a reported 11 million *rainbow trout*, and 2.5 million *brook trout* were imported into Canada from United States in 1972. These eggs and fingerlings came from Washington, Idaho, Montana and the New England states. The transformed fish across federal and provincial boundaries totaled approximately

14.6 million eggs and 4.8 million fry and fingerlings (Brown, 1983).

Imports:

Imports of cultured fish for food into Canada totaled to 986 MT. In addition to those

specified in 6234 kg of *carp* from Hong Kong, Taiwan and the United States territory, 909 kg

of *milkfish* from the Philippines and 978,950 of *trout* from Denmark, Great Britain, the United

States, Japan and Portugal. Most of the fish that were imported were frozen, but these

included also canned and smoked fish.

Marketing:

Aquaculturists in Canada have had no financial support, unlike what the government

has done to the agricultural fish hatching industry. The selling of game fish in Canada is of

recent origin and the little financial support offered to aquacultural farmers has been

oppressive to growth. The province of Quebec still prohibits the sale of Speckled *trout* for

human consumption. In the other provinces of Canada, there is great commercial *salmonoid*

fish. Other species that are grown are *char, salmon* and *trout*. The production and marketing

of *salmonoid* fish is dependent on the private individual farmers. There has been very little

government financial support to these individual farmers as stated earlier (Brown, 1983).

Live *trout* are sold sometimes for release into fishing waters are made on local and

regional basis. Sales of hatchery produced *Salmonoids*, mainly *rainbow trout* for human

consumption, are made in frozen form. The Canadian government has just allowed the transfer of fish from one locality to the next, until the Canadian provinces have been

depending on fish importation from Japan.

The feeding of fish has been on the average 1.4 MT for Salmonoids produced in

Canada. In Canada, there are both subsistence farmers who grow fish for their domestic use,

but there are also commercial fish producers (Brown, 1980).

Water Supply and Use:

Canada is blessed with abundant surface and ground waters, but yet only small

quantities are being used in fresh water fish aquaculture. There is significant emphasis placed

on the production of *Salmonoid* fish in Canada. The present hatcheries and rearing stations

are located on cold water sources. The Canadian water is reportedly hard. Although the

government in the country and private fish producers have experienced difficulty in locating

some hatchery sites with adequate groundwater discharge and yet most requirements for the

volume production of Salmonoids fish have been found. Some aquaculture procedures are

utilized in growing fish such as pothole lakes for live *trout* release and annual recovery basis.

Although cage culture has been used for commercial production of *Salmonoids* and other food

species in other countries; in Canada, it is still at the experimental stage except in the

province of Quebec which at present is serving the Montreal and New York markets.

Latin American Nations:

Aquaculture as food production is new in Latin America. Although aquaculture is

developing very fast today, 25 years ago, it played only a small role in the agricultural production in Latin American nations (Smith, 1982). At present, aquacultural production in

Latin America is low, but developing very fast and the number of commercial farms is very

low. There are no reliable statistical figures on current production. The major part of the

production is destined for local and subsistence consumptions. There are many restocking

programs, but Pillay (1976) suggests that 3.5% of food production is made up of *Mollusks*.

In El Salvador, Mexico and Ecuador, aquaculture is expanding very fast indeed. El Salvador

has an important marine shrimp fishery. It is supported by 14 processing plants with

combined capacity of 34 MT per day. *Shrimp* can be processed into several forms such as

block frozen tails or heads on animals, *butterfly* as the market needs might be. One feed mill

produces shrimp feed, its capacity is about 400 MT of feed per month.

Mexican *catfish* farm (Acuacultura Commercial's catfish) is on the road to Caimanero.

The farm is 68 hectares large (168 acres). Many farms have been started using this one as the

model. One farm owned by the government is located near Monterey in northeastern Mexico.

There is a private farm near Matomoros across the Rio Grande. There are many farms in the

State of Tamanlipas. These are operated by aquaculture cooperatives (Smith, 1982).

The operation at El Roasio is completely integrated. Eggs are produced on the farm

and fingerlings are kept in the pond. Where fingerlings reach four inches long, they are

placed in race ways. The *channel cat*, *Ictaturus Dunctutus*, are the species raised. The

temperature is hot all year around and so ten metric tons of *catfish* can be produced year

round.

When fish is harvested, it is placed on ice to be transported to the distribution centers

at La Piedant and Michoacan. These producers sell to wholesalers and mostly restaurants

(Pillay, 1976). This farm also sells fingerlings. These are sold to other farms or to the government. They have problems such as birds, like ducks. They have problems of poachers--thieves who steal fish. There are watchmen who keep watch over the premises round the clock.

Ecuador is a major *shrimp* producer in the America and reached a production of 26,100 MT in 1984. The rapid expansion of Ecuadorian *shrimp* led to the lowering of United States' shrimp prices in that year; 31-35 heads of shrimp were sold for one dollar (Conrad, 1990).

Rainbow trout farm is just south of Mexico City, along the boundary running east to west. Victor and Jaime Almazan are operating this *rainbow trout* farm. Today, two brothers have developed Rancho el Pedragal into Mexico's third or fourth largest trout ranch. They sell their products to ten Mexican states. They export their fresh fish to all major cities in Mexico. Apart from producing fresh fish, they have also made a factory which produces fish feeds. Some of these are used to feed their fish and some of them are sold to other fish farmers. They are also experimenting ways of producing fish eggs all year round. The Almazan brothers were the first ones to produce Coho Salmon on a commercial basis. When they first started, they sold all their *trout* to the exclusive restaurants in Mexico only, but now they are selling their fish almost everywhere in Mexico.

Cachama is the most popular freshwater fish in Venezuela. This specie has also been cultured in Brazil, Colombia, Panama, and in some of the Caribbean Islands. This fish can feed on plankton, wild fruits, nuts, wild rice, insects, molluscans; it will also eat farm produce like squash and other vegetables. *Cachama* can tolerate concentrations of dissolved oxygen for a short period of time. It reaches sexual maturity when three to four kilograms or about 55 cm in length. The eggs of this specie are very small. Hatchery operations for *cachama* are not complicated. Tanks are required for holding broods. It is because of the *Cachama's* characteristics that attracted the farmers to it (Ginnelly, 1990).

According to Swift (1977), Salaya and Martinez (1977), Gomez and Carvin (1979), Mexico, Venezuela, Colombia, Brazil, Peru, and Argentina produce a lot of *trout*. *Boco Chico, Coporo, Curimata* species are produced in Colombia and Brazil.

Brazil, Chile, and Argentina each produce a great deal of *mackerel*. Mexico and Brazil produce *Tilapia* fish. Mexico is also famous for *Bagre de Canal*. Mexico, Brazil, and Paraguay are famous for *Tilapia*. Honduras is known for freshwater *shrimp*. Colombia and Brazil are famous for *Muqilidos*. Mexico, Costa Rica, Panama, Brazil and Ecuador are known for *shrimp*.

African Nations:

Although the first signs of controlled fish production in Africa date back to the Pharaohs, any further development between then and now was not made toward fish farming. The first attempt to farm *Tilapia* date back to 1924 in Kenya, but aquaculture actually made its inroads after World War II. As a result, in the late 1950s there were about 300,000 fish ponds in Africa. The species that were cultured were *Tilapia* and aquaculture was considered to play a vital role in the food production strategy of many countries (Maar et al., 1966). After that time, development lost its momentum, mainly because *Tilapia* had many problems in its production. *Tilapia* have prolific reproduction that leads to over population and poor growth in ponds. *Tilapia* culture demands great managerial and entrepreneurial skills, which in many instances were lacking (Maar et al., 1966). After 1966, fish culture was revived through externally aided projects which are still in progress. Since 1972, over 30 external donors have carried out over 130 short or long term projects.

Despite the large efforts in public funding, aquaculture has not found its niche in African society, since African contribution to the global production is insignificant. Aquaculture production in Africa declined at an average rate of 13% per annum between 1980 to 1985 (FAO, 1985).

Egypt is a great producer of varieties of fish. But Egyptian aquaculture is not yet developed. Egypt's resources are drawn from about 13 million acres. This is twice the agricultural acreage. Commercial and subsistence fish come from the Nile, irrigation and drainage canals, lakes, sea coasts, and the high seas. Egypt produces 120 thousand tons of fish and most of it comes from freshwater. In 1954, the Ministry of Agriculture in Egypt began to use rice fields for fish farms. They produced *Tilapia* and *Cyprinus carpio*. They grew *Tilapia niloticus*, *Tilapia zillii*, and *Tilapia galilea*.

The species that are cultured in Tanzania are *Tilapia esculenta*, *T. rendalli*, *T. zillii*, *T. niloticus*, *T. pangami*, and *T. rukwensis*, etc. It was also discovered that *T. andersonii* did well in ponds in Zambia. It was expected that this same specie would do well in Tanzania. An experimental consignment was transferred from Zambia to Tanzania in 1968 (Anon, 1971).

In Zambia, efforts are now being put on the production of fish through fish farming to supplement production from the natural lakes and rivers. In the past, fish farming relied on extensive methods, but because of the demand for greater production from fish ponds, modern methods of intensive fish farming are being tried. At present, the Department of Fisheries operates experimental fish farms at Chilanga near Lusaka and at Mwekera near Kitwe and there are 14 other fish culture stations throughout the country (FAO, 1985).

At Mwakera, extensive production from the ponds averaged 185 kg per hectare per year. With fertilization the rate increased only to 820 kg per hectares per year. The constant flow of water through the ponds, the poor soil in some ponds and the accumulation of too much silt on the bottom without periodic clearing and drying inhibited high production. Some places in Zambia have high rates of natural production, such as Chipati, in the Eastern province and Solwezi in Northwest province, because of better soil while other places have poorer soils such as Serenje, Isoka and natural production is low. The three large ponds to which fertilizers only were added, were harvested after six months and gave a maximum production rate of 2, 5, 6 kg/ha/year.

In Nigeria, fish farming has been done at subsistence level for many years. Indeed fish farming in flood plains has been going on for a long time. However, modern fish farming practices were initiated a few years ago. In 1951, the Northern Nigerian Government started establishment of a fish farm at Ponyam near Jos, intending to cultivate the *common carp*. The digging of domestic fish ponds was encouraged by the Western and Eastern Governments. The development of salt water fish farming was started in the Niger Delta in 1965 by FAO, and the second project in Lagos in 1968 (FAO, 1968). Since that time fish ponds have developed all over Nigeria.

In Nigeria, fish pond construction is labor intensive, especially during the construction phase. Fish farming is a part-time work. It is estimated that 500,000 people are involved in aquaculture. Government experimental and demonstration fish farms are training extension staff who carry out surveys and supervision of pond construction and management.

Species of fish cultured in Nigeria are Tilapia species such as *T. niloticus, T. melanopleura, T. galilea* and *Cyprinus carpio* (Israel and European). There are three varieties: *Cyprinus capio, var specularis Cyprinus carpio var. Nundia,* and *Cyprinus carpio var communis.* In Nigeria also, farmers grow *Haterotis* species, *Labeo sp, Gymnarehus sp, Lates niloticus* (the Niger perch), and *Claris sp. Chrysichthys nigrodigitatus sp* (catfish).

Hemichromis fasciatus sp. Lutijanus spp., Gymnarchus spp., Elops spp., Heterotis spp., Ethmolosa fimbriala, Penaes duararum or Macrobrachium sp. and Mugil spp., a combination of carp plus mullets or Chrysichthys, plus Tilapia have been found to be ideal for polyculture (FAO, 1985).

In Malawi, fish culture is new. In all 200 hectares of ponds and reservoirs are cultivated, and they are producing about 50 tons of fish per year with other catches from sport fishing. The government has set up centers for production, pilot fish farms, and training of staff. Eleven hundred workers are employed in aquaculture and reservoir projects (FAO, 1985).

Sudan has over two million km^2, a coastline of 480 km and over 6400 km of river waters which cover about two million hectares. In the Sudd Region, at latitude 5-9° North along the White Nile, there is an area of about 100,000 km^2 comprising of permanent and temporary swamps. Apart from rivers, there are ponds, haffirs, reservoirs, and irrigation canals which range from a few thousand to a few million cubic meters, and depth of 1 to 20 m (Suna, 1975). In the Gezira scheme, the canal network is made up of 5649 km with depth ranging from 0.50 to 0.70 m. In the same way, there are other canals in Manigil Extension, Guneid Sugar Estate, and Kashm El Geirba projects.

Despite these vast areas of water, fish farming in Sudan are not able to produce fish protein in this great area of Western Sudan. In Kasaala and Gezira provinces, there are chronic shortages of meat due to the problems of the tsetse fly mainly in the Zeudi region. Other areas which are away from the location of the major fisheries are facing similar conditions (WHO, 1973).

All investigations carried out in Sudan have recommended fish farming as a remedy for these locations and it was because of this purpose that an experimental fish farm at Shangarm was established (Motabar, 1973). This farm was meant to develop the fish farming technology for the country. The lack of trained personnel and expertise in the field and inadequate planning have made this project impossible. Fish culture in Sudan is therefore still in its infancy (Motabar, 1973).

In South Africa, aquaculture in the 1980s was significant. The production rose from 345 tons to 3000 tons in 1988. This earned South Africa R.45 million. Seventy percent of all aquaculture undertakings were started only recently. Mussels now account for half of the total production in the country. *Trout* takes second place, accompanied by *water hawthorn*, *oysters* and *catfish*. In terms of value ornamental fish are third in bringing in foreign exchange (Wyrand Vys, Britz, Hecht, 1992).

The total production of fish farming compared to the total fisheries production is very small. The amount of fish farming within five years increased four times. The business owners in South Africa have to struggle with many factors in the surroundings, and the high energy nature of South African coastline, but the improvement that has been made is great and does suggest that success of fish farming is indeed possible.

In 1984, only three types--*rainbow trout*, *oysters*, and *water hawthorn*--were cultivated for human consumption on any appreciable scale. Six species of *fin* fish, one aquatic macrophyte and six species of mollusks are currently farmed on a commercial basis (De Moor, Bruton, 1989).

Perhaps the most significant thing occurred in 1982 when the Foundation for Research and Development of the Council for Scientific and Industrial Research chose an aquaculture working group to study the potential of fish farming in South Africa to determine the research needs of the industry. The organizational structures and the research supports have promoted fish culture industry throughout South Africa (Vys, Britz, Hecht, 1992).

CHAPTER II

"WEATHER AND CLIMATE"

Introduction

This chapter will discuss weather and climate of Africa and how each of these affect fish farming on the continent. We will discuss also types of species that can be grown on commercial scale under those geographical conditions.

Weather and Climate of Africa

Short term changes in atmospheric conditions are called weather, while other averages of weather conditions over a long period is known as climate.

Fish farmers must be aware of these short term and long term changes because they will affect their fish production. The type of fish, the duration of growth and the economic costs of fish farming will be greatly influenced by weather and climate. The aquaculturist should be fully aware how weather conditions change with the seasons and how much variation in weather can be expected from year to year.

An aquaculturist should be knowledgeable of the most important variables such as air temperature, solar radiation, cloud cover, wind velocity, rainfall, and evaporation (Boyd, 1990).

Solar Radiation

Solar radiation is influenced by atmosphere transparency, time taken for photoperiod to take place and the angle of elevation of the sun. The atmospheric transparency is affected by dust, clouds, water vapor and the distance the light takes to reach earth's surface.

Because the distance between the sun and the earth's surface is shortest within the tropics closest to the equator, thus the amount of the solar radiation is greatest at the equator (Boyd, 1990). The length of the daily (throughout the year) light is longest along the equator (12 hours). However the greatest length of daylight increases with increasing latitude. This is usually more than 12 hours for only a certain portion of the year in spring and summer. Higher latitudes receive less radiation than lower ones. Solar radiation will be affected by the cloud cover. Places having dense atmospheric pollution will receive low radiation.

In Africa, air temperatures are high, as most of Africa, both North and South lie within the tropics. These conditions above are very characteristic in Africa. In Africa, atmospheric pollution is less dense than in temperate regions which have heavy industrial technology. In some parts of Africa mainly along the deserts, there will be heavy dust cover as a result of sand blown into the atmosphere by the strong desert winds. These desert winds will blow but occasionally. The time when these winds are calm, the atmosphere will be clear and will allow very high solar radiation. This is the case in African deserts. They have very high temperatures most of the year due to the clear sky. Air temperatures will also be affected by altitudes. Places with high altitudes, air temperatures prevail. At low altitudes, air temperatures will be higher. It is hotter at the foot of mountains, and at sea-level than it will be on top of high mountains.

Effects of Solar Radiation to Fish Farming

Africa as a whole lies within tropical and sub-tropical regions in which case it has generally very high temperatures everywhere on the continent. Solar radiation is very high. This affects fish farming on the continent, as temperature influences fish farming in many aspects. But in Africa the air temperature is high and so in most places on the continent fish farming is possible providing that precipitation which will be necessary for water in ponds, is adequate.

In most places of the continent, except in deserts and semi-deserts, water is available. Once water is available and temperatures are high, then fish farming is possible. This necessitates the discussion of the climate of Africa.

Climate

Climate, according to Hance (1975), is the most important physical factor which retards economic development. Africa lies astride the equator and the distances from the equator to the North and South are almost equal. Tunis is 2,400 miles and Cape Town is 2,600 miles away from the equator. The location of the continent is indicative that temperatures are high over the bulk of the continent. The element of the climate that is significant is rainfall. Precipitation is classified into numerous systems such as tropical rainfall. This is marked by a 10 to 12 months rainfall. This type of rainfall makes some locations too wet to be of any utility. But the combination of high temperature and high rainfall makes Africa a region of great potential productivity. In such a location aquaculture would thrive very well. Fresh, warm water is significant to the fish farmers. Apart from water supply, the solar radiation is also high and yet temperatures are very influential and significant to fish farming productivity.

The regions of subtropical climate are relatively small, and their utilizable portions are further restricted by difficult land form conditions.

92% of the continent may be said to suffer from climatic disability. It had a problem of water. Some portions of the continent have too much water that they do not know what to do with it and yet in some parts where water is needed is non-existent.

Vegetation

About 27% of Africa is forested. But much of the total area is in Savannah woodlands. The wood in Africa are of little utility. These trees are not suitable for lumbering. It should be noted that rainforests remain as very important resource which may be put to use in future than it is done today. Trees such as pines and eucalyptus grow with great rapidity in extensive areas, but each region of Africa has different surface cover.

Hydrology

The most significant aspect of hydrology on the impact of economic development are the navigability of streams and other inland waters. The control of surface water and the tapping of underground water for portable waters and irrigation or wetland cultivation and the developing of the rivers for hydroelectric power is very significant.

The aspect of significance in this case relates to fish farming and aquatic animal resources. In rivers and lakes, there are animals such as hippos, which are important for their meat, crocodiles for their skins, and other types of fish for their meat, all these are affected by the presence or absence of water. Water bodies are also vital for many other reasons apart from fish farming, but these are not vital for our discussions here.

Some aquifers are too saline and some of the underground waters are of fossil origin and can be used but only few times. Some irrigation communities use water more rapidly than it can be replaced. This is the case in respect to Nile, Maghreb, the Senegal, the upper Niger, Share, Logone, Tana, Rufiji, Zambezi, and orange rivers. There are substantial opportunities for development of these resources, but no rapid extension is to be expected because of the high capital costs involved (Hence, 1975).

Such locations where temperatures are moderate throughout the year, precipitation high, vegetation good and hydrology appropriate would be very favorable for pond fish farming. This is not the case in Africa. Because of all places discussed in chapter one, Africa is least productive. It is appropriate at this juncture to discuss the systems in use and species cultivated in fish farming in Africa.

Systems in Use and Species Cultivated on the Continent

Despite the fact that pond fish farming started in Africa 2500 B.C. (Kigeya, 1995), fish farming in Africa remains at subsistence level and has not found a niche on the continent as a whole.

The aquaculture in Africa has ancient origins, yet the introduction of more conventional fish farming systems is encumbered by an array of difficulties. It is very clear that these difficulties can be overcome. Before an attempt is made to discuss the difficulties, we need to discuss the fish farming systems.

Aquaculture on this continent has been discussed several times in FAO World Symposium, and more recently at the FAO World Fisheries Conference, Rome, and during Aquaculture 84 (Commonwealth Secretariat, 1988). Much of the information regarding fish farming in Africa is based on reports and papers that have been presented in these conferences.

Some of the countries involved in these conference reports were Zambia (FAO, 1980), Ivory Coast (Vincke, 1982), Mozambique (FAO, 1982), Rwanda (Schmidt and Vincke, 1981), Central Africa Republican (Blessech, et al., 1983), Malawi (Cross, et al., 1983), Tunisia (FAO, 1983), Congo (Balarin, 1983), Egypt (Sodek, 1984) and a current FAO 12 country review by Balarin (1984, a-g) and Balarin (1985, h-l) (Commonwealth Secretariat, 1983).

It has already been mentioned that fish culture started in Egypt about 2500 B.C., but organized aquaculture efforts on the continent started only recently after the Second World War (Meschkat, 1967). The exploitation of fish from lakes, rivers, and seas has been going on from very early times. Because people were accustomed to harvesting fish from these water bodies freely and whenever they needed it, fish farming did not take root in Africa until the 1950s and 1960s.

The traditional fish farming techniques were left only on a few spots of Africa. Fish culture proper was introduced on the continent during the colonial period. The main emphasis was placed on rearing and stocking of sport fisheries. It was soon realized that there was a need to increase fish farming through reservoir stocking, and through classical pond culture in

1924 (Balarin, 1979). But the actual scientific fish farming approach was put in place only after the Second World War. By 1960, there were about 300,000 ponds operating on the whole continent of Africa (Anon, 1984).

Fish farming development in Africa falls into two main categories: (1) The small scale rural aquaculture. This is characteristic of rural development by individual farmers, artisanal, village or community groups using unsophisticated techniques for the purpose of having more food in the community. This system was usually integrated along with other farming systems. This fish farming system was part-time rather than a full-time venture. Farmers had one or two ponds, but still carrying out the production of coffee, bananas, cotton, animal husbandry like cattle, pigs, goats and the like. (2) Large Scale Aquaculture Industry generally developed as private sector investment or government cooperate activity, involving large capital outlay, centralized management and a certain degree of vertical integration whose objective is return on the investment. The whole system involves difficult feasibility study for correct system, species and site choice depends on inputs to maximize yields.

The initial emphasis was placed on commercial enterprises for rural people. They marketed fish like trout and black bass. Most of the African countries did only subsistence fish farming. Of all countries, the most important countries for fish farming are Zaire, Madagascar, Kenya, Central African Republic, Egypt, Cameroon, and the Congo where 85.6% of ponds were recorded and 38% were in Zaire alone.

Large scale industrial aquaculture has not developed to any large extent, for economic reasons.

In the whole of African continent, there are 10-15 public or private commercial enterprises, there are about 13-20 pilot projects not yet economically viable and many projects are still at planning stages (Coche, 1983).

Twenty-three countries on the continent report large scale activities, but yet only few are actually producing the fish. These are the *tilapia* farms in Ivory Coast, Kenya, Malawi, Nigeria and Egypt; trout farms in Kenya and Zimbabwe; Machrobrachium projects in Mauritius and Zimbabwe; and oyster farms in Senegal. The largest project are planned for Egypt (1000 ha), Angola (500 ha), Lesotho (350 ha), Upper Volta (450 t), Libya (700 t); Madagascar (200 ha); and Kenya for various types (Commonwealth Secretariat, 1988).

Most of the countries in Africa report freshwater culture practices. Mariculture activities have started only recently and there is a trend of making use of brackish waters.

Fish Farming Aims and Objectives

There are enumerable aims and objectives of fish farmers in pursuing fish culture on the continent. Some of the aims and objectives are as follows:

(1)   The major objective of fish farmers is the production of fish for domestic food consumption;

(2)   Production of fish for fishery stocking.

(3)   Production of varieties of species with the intentions of perpetuating species that will in future be used for planting;

(4)   Production of bait for commercial or sport fishing;

(5)   Production of ornamental or aquarium fish;

(6)   Recycling of organic wastes, such as in sewage oxidation ponds;

(7)   Rearing of select fish for stocking waterways for aquatic weed control as well as to central vectors of such diseases as malaria or bilharzia; and

(8)   Production of trash fish as a constituent of animal feeds (Commonwealth Secretariat, 1985).

Most governments in Africa are working hard to increase fish production, by either training young people who can be used to help farmers in rural areas or by introducing new varieties of fish in Africa. Private farmers are trying their best with limited financial resources and knowledge of fish farming. The more encouragement the private farmers receive from the government, the more they are motivated to put in more time and resources into fish farming projects. What is most annoying is the fact that years pass by, but the statistics of fish farming in Africa never changes. It is quite appropriate at this juncture to discuss the systems of fish farming on the continent of Africa.

Fish Farming Systems

Fish farming in Africa has long history, originating from the African Kings (pharaohs) in Egypt 2500 BC (Kigeya, 1995).

In Africa, there are varieties of fish farming systems and can be categorized as:

(i)   Capture fish farming versus indigenous systems. Fish farming in Africa can be classified in two categories and these are capture versus pond fish farming. The difference between the two is essentially the stocking method. In a capture system, eggs, larvae or adult fish enter the water body during the time of filling and the quantitative regulation by man is non-existent. It is true, however, that in some cases, man may want to plant particular types of fish and then quantitative regulation of stocking may occur. This type of fish farming is common in rice-fields and tidal ponds which are numerous in Southeast Asia. We have a few examples in Madagascar, Mauritius and in a few other parts of the continent, where rice fields do exist. On the other hand, cultural systems which also are referred to as indigenous, the stocking of fish ponds, dams, lakes, rivers, is controlled on the basis of size of the fish to be stocked, the age which the farmer may consider appropriate, or sex which the producer may desire to have in that water body.

(ii)   Subsistence versus commercial. In the industrialized countries of Europe and North America, fish farming is a purely commercial and the practices used are on large scale. But in developing countries of Africa, aquaculture or fish farming per se is for subsistence. Fish in Africa is grown, in most parts for domestic use and on rare cases for commercial purposes. This is true in all parts of sub-Saharan Africa, except South Africa, where fish farming, aquaculture is practiced for commercial purposes. In the last twenty years, many foreign companies have made contracts with African governments and changing this trend in many parts of the continent. In most parts of Africa, commercial fish farming is very poorly developed (CIFA, 1983). Subsistence fish farming is usually carried out in small stagnant ponds which require low inputs and serves the objective of family nutrition.

(iii)   Level of integration in such cases as monocultures whereby a single specie or a single sex is practiced. Both stagnant and flow-through or recirculation systems are used. On the other hand, polycultures in which mixtures of fish species in the same production unit are kept. Each specie sticks to their own specific food preferences or habitat and do not compete with each other for food or space. Polyculture is mainly practiced in stagnant ponds but also in systems with limited water exchange like tidal ponds.

(iv)   Integrated fish farming is practiced in agriculture and animal husbandry component, e.g., rice-cum-fish and duck-cum-fish culture. In these systems, fish culture is applied for the purposes of utilizing the waste products of other components (Pullin & Shehadeh, 1980). Integrated fish farming is practiced in ponds with little or not water exchange (Huisman, 1985).

It is important at this time to discuss the species cultivated on the African continent.

Species Cultivated in Africa

The major species cultivated in Africa could be divided into two main groups:

indigenous and exotic. The indigenous species were very minimally known, because when

fish farming started in Kenya in 1924, the fishery experts had no biological knowledge of fish

in lakes. The fish farming experts utilized exotic species and they introduced these into lakes, rivers, dams, reservoirs and ponds. The types of fish the experts introduced into the lakes added to those which were there already (Balarin, 1985). The breeding that took place was between the indigenous and the exotic types.

Of all the species in ponds, lakes and rivers, only five could be considered indigenous, namely, *Protopterus, Bagrus, O. esculentus, O. variabilis* and *Mormyrus* (Kigeya, 1995). The biggest number of fish in ponds, rivers, dams and reservoirs are either exotic or hybridized species. These came from outside the continent and were stocked in ponds, rivers, dams and lakes. Such species were foreign to Africa although they resulted from the mixture of exotic and indigenous species. This was true in Kenya, Uganda, Tanzania, and many other Central African nations.

Mirror Carp was introduced to Africa from Israel in 1957 (Balarin, 1985). Other species that are cultivated in Africa include Oreochromis niloticus, O. leucostictus, *Tilapia* zillii which was considered inappropriate because of its slow growth and small size (Semakula & Makoro, 1967). Species such as *O. mossambicus, O. hornrum* were brought to Uganda from Zanzibar, *O. aureus* from Israel, *O. niger* from Britain, *O. niloticus* from Lake Rudolf in Kenya, and *T. rendelli* in Kenya and *Procambrus spp.* in Kenya and Uganda. These species are mainly sold to Kampala Hotels in Uganda because of their good quality.

In Egypt, there are species such as *Tilapia* niloticus, *Tilapia* zillii, and *Tilapia* galilea. These were used in rice fields, canals, dams and then spread everywhere in Egypt in the long run. Other species that are grown in East Africa are *Tilapia* esculentus, T. rendalli, T. zillii, T. niloticus, T. pangani and *T. rukwensis* are commonly cultivated in the eastern nations of Africa.

Zambia produces a great deal of *Chipati*, and other various types of *Tilapia* species.

In Nigeria, *Tilapia* species such as *T. niloticus, T. melonopleura, T. galilea, Cyprinus carpio*

from Israel and some other European nations. There are other *Tilapia* species that are grown

in Nigeria and these are *Cyprinus carpio* var. *specularis, Cyprinus carpio* var. *nundia* and

Cyprinus carpio var. *communis*. In Nigeria also farmers grow *Haterotis species, Labeo*

species, Gymnarchus sp., Lates niloticus, Clarias sp., Chrysichthys nigrodigitatus sp. (catfish),

Hemichromis fasciatus, Lutijanus spp, Gymnarchus spp., Elops spp., Heterotis spp., Ethmolosa

fambriala, Panaes duorarum or *Machrobrachium sp.*, and *Mugil spp*. A combination of carps

plus mullets or Chrysichthys plus *Tilapia* have been found to be ideal for polyculture in West

Africa (FAO, 1985).

In South Africa, farmers very frequently grow *Mussels*, which account for half of the

country's total production. *Trout* take second place, accompanied by *water hawthorn, oyster*

and *catfish*. In terms of value ornamental fish are third in bringing in foreign exchange in the

country (Kigeya, 1995).

Apart from the types of fish species that are commonly grown in Africa, there are also

characteristics of certain types of fish that are commonly selected for cultivation. It is

important at this time to briefly consider and discuss characteristics of fish that are desirable

among farmers on the African continent in general.

Types of Fish Usually Grown in Africa

Usually farmers in Africa are helped by extension workers to assist them in selecting

the more useful and economical varieties of fish that can be grown in Africa. These types are selected in accordance to the benefits they offer to the fish farmers. These could be classified into: (i) those which can withstand the climate of the region in which it will be raised; (ii) those whose rates of growth is sufficiently high; (iii) those which can successfully reproduce under the conditions of rearing; (iv) those which thrive on the abundant artificial food and prove satisfactory to the farmer to support high population density into the ponds, and (v) those that are resistant to disease (Huet, 1992).

Adaptation to Climate

This is a very vital point which limits the use of both warm and cold water species. *Salmonids* which are cold water fish cannot tolerate warm water due to the absence of oxygen content. Rearing of *Salmonids* is therefore limited to temperate regions or to mountain waters which are sufficiently cold in tropical climates.

In the same way, tropical fish such as *Tilapia* of Africa and *mud carp* of southern China, cannot survive in temperate climates, where winter temperatures are too cold for them. But these types can be kept in ponds which can be heated in winter seasons if necessary (Huet, 1992). *Tilapia* and *Tilapia* spp. are the types of fish that are suited to the climates of Africa. It is no wonder that *Tilapia* is the most cultivated fish on the continent of Africa.

Rate of Growth

Fish intended for food must reach full size rapidly. Thus, small sized species such as *Gasterosteus* in Europe and the *Haplochronius* of Africa. Because these types of fish take long to mature, they are not commonly grown in Africa, as they cannot reproduce well in ponds.

Reproduction under Conditions of Cultivation

It is necessary that fish should reproduce in captivity and that they can do this without needing special conditions which must be fulfilled. They should also give a high return in eggs and fry. A fish that does not meet these conditions cannot be domesticated in Africa. *Barbus* and *Citharimus* of Africa grow well in ponds, but do not reproduce sufficiently enough as to give farmers enough profit; and therefore these two types of fish are occasionally reared. *Tilapia*, on the other hand, reproduce profusely, so much so that farmers are encouraged to keep them in their ponds because of the profits they bring. Other farmers on the continent do complain that *Tilapia* reproduces excessively much more than what the farmers can care for. This is one of the disadvantages of *Tilapia* spp. and as such artificial controls are created to keep *Tilapia*'s too much reproduction in check.

Aptitude to Artificial Food

It is important to realize that if fish farming is to develop to any meaningful pedestal, fish farmers need to be trained. In the course of this training, it is good to help them to understand that the high production rate of fish depends on how the fish accept the abundant artificial food. The type of fish that fulfills this condition permits high production rate reaching or passing the ten tons per year (Bronon, 1977). It is also necessary to make the farmers realize that the maximum profit will only accrue if the most economical feeds are utilized to feed the fish in ponds. The most economical feed will be the natural ones, but usually these do not result into maximum production rate in fish. It is probably the reason why most farmers turn to artificial feeds which would result into maximum production of fish. It is the reason why African farmers stick to *Tilapia* spp. which can produce profusely yet depending on natural feeds instead of artificial ones. *Tilapia* becomes the most popular species of fish for growth, because it will use natural foods which will not be too costly to farmers and at the same time produce profusely. If *Tilapia* fish is fed on artificial feeds, it will produce more than when it is fed on natural feeds. But this will not be necessary as the fish produces profusely enough for the farmers to want no more. Because *Tilapia* feeds on local foods and results into maximum production, it has become the most favored species in Africa.

The Taste Value of Fish for Eating

It is also important for farmers to understand that reared fish should suit the taste of consumers. Certain catfish introduced in Europe *(Letalurus melas)* which breeds and grows easily in ponds are considered most unsuitable for consumers. Certain species, however, called *(Osphronemus goramy)* are known as gourmet in Indonesia and they are very much preferred by the consumers.

Tilapia is a tasty type of fish in Africa and very much appreciated by the farmers as it is very economical and very manageable by all farmers in Africa.

Population Density in Fish Farming

Fish farmers need to understand that good fish for rearing should be able to assure sufficient dense population. The last species are those which are social and gregarious (Huet, 1992). Certain catfish such as pike will only accept a dense population to a certain age; six to eight weeks, over that age, they devour each other thus ruining the economic returns.

Tilapia species is one famous African species that is known for prolific reproduction and this among some farmers around the world find it as a liability. The more fish there are in the pond, the more food they will eat. It will necessitate supplementary feeding to accommodate the tilapia dense population. But looking at it from an economic point of view, the more fish there are in the pond, the more profit the farmers expect to receive. The fish may consume additional food, but the returns will also be rewarding. Thus *Tilapia*, Mirror Carp, Lates niloticus, Mussels in South Africa, are very important species in Africa because they reproduce a great deal and keep dense population and as a result the economic returns are excellent.

Resistance to Disease

Fish that is fit for cultivation should be resistant to disease and should be able to accept handling without difficulty. Thus, *Tilapia*, Mirror carps, Lates niloticus, Mussels allow any handling without too much discomfort or distress. It is the reason why many African farmers find it easy to deal with them.

Tilapia species is the most preferred on the continent of Africa and in many other

tropical countries such as those in Latin America and in southeast Asia. It is vital at this

point to discuss more about *Tilapia* species and what makes it so special.

Tilapia Specie

Many fish farmers in Africa complain that they are experiencing shortages of tilapia

fry for stocking and restocking ponds, dams, rivers, reservoirs and other water bodies. The

production of *Tilapia* has been increased by separating the fry and fingerlings from the on-

growing and fattening stages. This increased tremendously the new techniques for improving

Tilapia reproduction rates. It has also added to the amount of fry produced per female or

per ^{m2} of hatchery (Commonwealth Secretariat, 1985). *Tilapia* belongs to the perciformes and

to the cichlidae family. *Tilapia* forms a genus of fish found in the intertropical waters of

Africa (Huet, 1992). *Tilapia* are robust fish which can withstand high water temperatures.

They are an easy type of fish to transport which would account to the easy dispersion of

Tilapia spp. to different locations. *Tilapia* are warm water fish. They can survive in very

high atmospheric heat in summer. They can withstand any temperatures between 12°C-35°C.

Some *Tilapia* species such as *T. sparmani,* are as low as 8°C. *T. mossambicus* and *Timlotica*

can also stand temperatures as low down as 8°C (Huet, 1992).

Tilapia is so popular among African farmers because it does well in fresh clear warm

water, just as it does in brackish water. *Tilapia* fish can be divided into two major groups:

(i) herbivorous and (ii) *Microphytagous* and *omnivorous groups* of the species with lower reproductive possibilities and practices month incubation. The main species in this group are *T. macrochiri*, *T. mossambicus*, *T. nilotica* and *T. nigra*.

Some species such as *T. sparrmari*, *T. galilea*, *T. leudeloti*, *T. andersonii*, *T. esculenta*, and *T. leucosticta* are not popular among fish farmers in Africa.

T. massambica originated in the east and south of Africa. Then it spread into Far East in Java and into the Indonesia Islands, in Malaysia, and Taiwan (Huet, 1992).

They were then spread to Thailand, then Antilles and into south of United States. *T. rendalli* originated in tropical Africa. It then spread to Zaire and into Uganda, Kenya, Tanzania and Rwanda.

T. macrochir originated in the southern part of Central Africa. Since 1947, it has been very popular in Zaire and in many parts of Africa. *T. nigre* is grown in Kenya, but *T. nilotica* does better in West Africa. *Hemichromis fasciatus* is not of *Tilapia species* and is used much to keep *tilapia* prolific reproduction into balance. *Hemichromis fry* must be produced in separate ponds in which one or more pairs of *Hemichromis* are placed. These species protect their young until they are 20 mm. *Serranochromis* have been studied a great deal in Zaire at Katanga. They are important for controlling predators.

Haplochromis mellandi was used in Zaire at Katanga as controller for molluses. They keep *bilharziasis* down and they are being used in various countries of Africa for bilharziasis control (Huet, 1992).

Reproduction of *Tilapias*

Tilapias make their nests at the bottom of the ponds. The female spawns in the nests made by the male. These *tilapia* species particularly of *Microphagous* type such as *T. mossambicus* and *Macrochir*, protect their young ones in their mouths. They practice mouth incubation. But *T. melanopluera* and *Sparmani* do not practice mouth incubation. The males have two openings under their belly one is the anus and the other is urogenital opening. The female tilapia on the other hand has three openings: the anus, the genital and the urinary opening (Pillay, 1993).

Tilapia become adult in the second six months of their existence. The size depends on the species, the quantity of natural food found in the area and the size of the space where the fish can play. For most fish, temperatures play a big role in their reproduction. The average temperatures during the spawning period should be between 20° to 21° C. In the equatorial region where it is always warm, spawning goes on throughout the year. In temperate regions, however, *Tilapias* do not spawn in winters. In warm regions such as those of Africa, they spawn in 5 to 7 week intervals (Huet, 1992).

Construction of the Nest

The male constructs the nests, and the shape of each differs according to the species. *T. Macrochir* construct their nests at the bottom of the pond, at a depth of between 30 and 150 cm or 1 to 5 feet. The diameter of the rest varies from 50-200 cm (2 to 8 feet). The nest is usually circular and complex. It looks like a trunk of a cone, the upper face looks like a concave.

T. Mossambicus constructs a nest which is similar to that of Macrochir. But its nest is simpler than that of Macrochir. It looks like a simple bowl. *T. melanopleura* spawns in shallow water either on a rather steep bank of 45 to 60°. It is made of from 5 to 10 hemispheric holes of 8 to 12 cm in diameter (Huet, 1992). *T. melanopleura* constructs its nest in the sides of the banks of the ponds while *T. macrochir* prepares its next at the bottom of the pond.

When the male completes constructing the nest, the female lays the eggs in it and they are fertilized. After spawning, *tilapia* keeps her eggs and protects them from danger. Some of them keep the eggs in their mouths or practice mouth incubation. This continues until they are hatched (Pillay, 1993).

The eggs of *T. melanopleura* measure about 2-5 mm in diameter. They are laid in one of the holes of the nest. They stick one to the other on the upper side of the hole. After spawning, the female stands in guard over the hole to ward off the predators. Usually she takes a position in the nest with its head sticking out. After spawning and fertilization those eggs of *T. mossambicus* and *T. macrochir*, etc., who practice mouth incubation, protect their eggs by keeping them in the their mouths.

The number of eggs depends on the species and size of the brood. For each spawning, there are about hundreds or even thousands of eggs at most (Huet, 1992). The eggs are hatched 6 days after spawning. After hatching the fry are still protected by their parents. As the fry grow they begin to disperse, and at the end of 10-12 days, they are completely disintegrated. The fry now swim around in shoals (Huet, 1992).

Feeding and Growth of *Tilapia*

Some *Tilapias* feed on micro-organisms while others are herbivorous. *T. mossambicus* are omnivorous and plankton eaters. *T. melanopleura* are phytophagous. They feed on filamentous algae and aquatic plants. They prefer submerged, semi-submerged or floating vegetation. They also go for emergent plants. *T. macrochir* is a fish which feeds on small micro-organisms, plankton and biological cover. Most *Tilapias* feed on insect larvae, crustaceans (Huet, 1992). *Tilapias* ponds will do well if they feed on artificial food. This should be at a later date. At the early age, *Tilapias* would do better if they feed on natural food which will be increased by fertilization of the pond. When the fry reach 4 to 5 cm they start taking artificial food. *Tilapias* can be fed with plants, farinaceous vegetation and many other wastes, domestic and otherwise. Plants are suitable for the herbivorous and farinaceous food is good for all species (Pillay, 1993).

The farinaceous foods are usually meal waste, cassava bran and flour. Industrial wastes, domestic wastes such as decomposed fruits, brewery draft, coffee pulp, and wastes from local beverages are all useful as *Tilapia* food. All species of *Tilapia* like eating termites. If fish are fed regularly, production can be increased to up to about 10 times (Pillay, 1993).

Growth

The growth of *tilapia* varies according to the species and also in accordance to individual fish. The growth also will depend on the type of food available, both natural and artificial. In rich waters, the growth is faster. The temperatures are also very important to fish growth. In open amounts of water, large fish will reach lengths of 40 cm and weighs around about 1200 to over 1300 gm.

If you want to produce fish for sale, the fish should be at least 20 cm or weigh about 150-200 gms. *T. Macrochir* and *T. Melanopleura* reach these sizes after 10 or 11 months, but this is not the case when the water is poor. In poor water, the same species will not even weight 100 gm in one year (Huet, 1992). Males grow faster generally than female species.

Rearing Fry of Different Sizes

Multiple ages of fish together in ponds can do very well. The pond is stocked with fish of all ages. This is done right from fry to broodfish. This is known as the mixed method. The aim is to produce fish of all sizes in as great quantity as possible.

If the fish are properly fed, it will give the fish great opportunity to produce as much as possible. But if such method is applied to *Tilapia* with their prolific production, leads to overproduction and as a result sizes are sacrificed. this will also hinder genetic improvement (Pillay, 1993). Sometimes fish of different sizes can be reared together but for a short time. The fish are allowed to grow together, fed together and allowed to fatten and reproduce one time only. The pond can be dried when the fry hatched in the pond are ready to be planted in another pond.

When the fish pond is drained, the old fish are sold for food and the fry are carried into another pond. This method has the advantage of producing fish of the same size, but the weight production will be much smaller than in the previous method of multiple rearing of the fish with different sizes. This method is not very popular.

Another method of rearing *Tilapia* is separate by age group in different ponds. Spawning and rearing young fry are done in spawning ponds only for production of fry which are sufficiently large enough so as to be released into the fattening ponds. The reproduction ponds are just spawning ponds and are smaller than 1/40th of an acre. One species of *Tilapia* should be raised in each reproduction pond. They are harvested when young fish are 4 cm or 1-5/8 in. They can reach this size in two months. This will also depend on water quality and the amount of food that can be found in the environment.

In the growing ponds, the aim is to produce as soon as possible the fish which will weigh about 100 gm. This complicates the problem when it comes to *Tilapia* species which reproduces when they are about 10 cm or 4 in. in water which is poor in quality. If fish is to grow as fast as possible, they must be abundantly fed. When the fish grows fast they will also be big in size.

Tilapia with Controlled Reproduction

To control unnecessary *Tilapia* reproduction, predators must be added. These predators continually keep the *Tilapia* prolific reproduction in check. This works in respect to *Hemichronmis fasciatus*. It was tried in Zaire and Comeroun. *Lates niloticus* in Nigeria and *Micropterus salmoides* in Madagascar (Huet, 1986).

The method of controlling *Tilapia* reproduction is a delicate one because sometimes, the predator is too brutal in its actions and reduces the fry too much that they will not be enough. Sometimes, the predator may be less active that the reproduction will not be reduced as required. This will lead into loss of weight to the reared fish as a result of too much

population in the pond.

<u>Monosex Cultivation</u>

The problem of premature production of *Tilapia* can be avoided if the cultivated fish

in the pond are of one sex only. Male *Tilapia* grow more rapidly than females and two

methods are possible. Fish are sorted out according to sex rather early, then males are

separated from females and are grown in different ponds. One needs to be very careful so

that no mistake is made during sorting period. If one small mistake is made, it will upset the

whole operation. The method can be used well by experienced farmers, assisted by

experienced personnel.

CHAPTER III

PROMOTING FISH PRODUCTIVITY IN PONDS

The main objective for keeping fish in ponds is the production of fish in great quantity, such that the farmer can sell them and make profit. There are three principle objectives for cultivation of fish, namely: (i) quantity, (ii) quality and (iii) economic production.

All fish farmers wherever they are, their major aim in cultivating fish in ponds is to produce great quantity of fish for eating for selling and restocking. Quantitative production means production that will allow the fish to grow well and have weight that will be acceptable to the consumers. In Africa, this is accomplished by growing Tilapia, mixing the age groups. This will allow the farmer to have fish of various sizes, some big and some medium size. This will allow the producer to have fish all the time in the pond.

Commercial fish farmers produce fish of good quality which will attract buyers and increase the economic value of the stock. This is accomplished in Africa by growing of fish of the same size and age in a pond. When harvesting is done, all fish will have uniform weight and will be more impressive to the consumers. These are likely to be better and bigger than those that are of different ages and sizes during the growing period.

Economic Production

Fish farmers intend to produce as many fish as possible. The number will have to be accompanied by the quality of fish. If the fish are many and qualitative, the farmer will have to raise his prices and, as a result, profit from the whole stock will be promoted.

Method of production could be semi-intensive; intensive and extensive. This will depend on the type of feeding the farmer is using. If a farmer uses natural foods only or natural and artificial used together or if artificial food is used by itself, fish in ponds will tend to grow faster and the quality will be promoted. If natural food is used, the fish, particularly Tilapia, they will be many in the pond. But they may not be as qualitative as those fish that are fed on artificial food. Artificial food has nutrients that are needed for the proper production of the stock, but it is costly. In some cases, natural and artificial foods should be used to feed the fish in ponds. Some fish, such as *carp*, can be raised on artificial feed. But for economic purposes natural foods should be 50% and the artificial food 50%. By so doing, the farmer will economize value of the stock.

Major Food Used on Ponds

The main feeds distributed on fish farms are pulse food, e.g., soya, lupin and grains such as maize, cereals, leaves, land plants which are distributed to herbivorous fish. A variety of feed stuff are being used in feeding *Tilapia* fish in Africa, including plant leaves, rice-bran, oil seeds, oil cakes, copra wastes, manioc and brewery remains.

Some farmers in some parts have used chicken diets, and sometimes is mixed with protein rich ingredients. There are other inexpensive feeds tried in Africa such as copra meal, cotton seed oil cake, these are used in Central African Republic and wheat flour, cattle blood meal. If all these feeds are tried by some farmers, fish farming in Africa would find its niche. In Ivory Coast, fish farmers have been using rice-polishings, wheat middlings, peanut oil, cake, fish meal and oyster shell. Each *Tilapia* species has its feed preferences.

T. Massambica are omnivorous and plankton eaters. *T. melanopleura* are phytophagous, feeding on filamentous algae, and aquatic plants. They prefer submerged semi-submerged or floating vegetation. They also eat emergent plants whose stalks are not ligneous. *T. Macrochir* is a species that feed on small micro-organism, plankton and biological cover. Most *Tilapia* feed on insect larvae, crustaceans and detritus.

If fish in ponds are fed regularly, with the type of feed they prefer, no doubt fish production will be increased and sometimes to even ten times.

Methods of Increasing Fish Production

Whether production is quantitative, qualitative or economic, there are many ways of controlling and increasing output. these could be classified as biological or non-biological.

1.   **Non-Biological Methods:**

   (a)   General technical and sanitary means: If a fish farm is to be run normally, then technical and sanitary measures must be strictly observed.

      (i)   Different age groups of fish must be kept in the pond,

      (ii)   Enough oxygen content must be ensured in the pond at all times. The machines and the people to observe this must be in place all

Hi-baller

Mechanical Weed Cutter

the time. If fish lose oxygen, they will die instantly or they will

be stressed to the point of death,

(iii)   Special precautions should be taken against diseases. There are

various diseases which attack fish. Some of these are introduced

from outside the country. If any disease is observed, it should

be dealt with before it spreads to other locations. There are

many diseases that attack fish, but these will be discussed in a

later chapter. Suffice it to say, that disease must be eradicated

from the farm, if fish farming can be promoted (Huet, 1986).

2. Maintenance and Improvement of Ponds: Apart from the upkeep of dikes,

banks and the quality of the water, but also action against excessive water plants must be

strictly observed. At times excessive plants in the pond will utilize the oxygen and fish will

not have enough oxygen and eventually they will die. Excessive water plants can be

detrimental in respect to fish in the pond. Water plants can occupy the space where the fish

would have laid eggs. And sometimes, fish can be caught into these plants that they will die.

When the fish farmer comes to harvest the pond, excessive water plants can prevent a net

from being used in the pond. It is therefore important to watch against excessive plants. It is

true that these water plants act as food for fish in the pond, but when these plants are

excessive, they will cause greater problems than the goodness they serve.

It is not judicious to advocate complete eradication of plants from the pond, but should

not be left to be too excessive. These water plants can be removed by mechanical means by

cutting or by chemical means whereby chemicals in reasonable quantity are poured on the pond to only destroy the weeds but not to destroy the animals in the water. This chemical means approach should not be used by an inexperienced individual. This can result into killing all fish in the pond, if the amount of chemicals are not measured wisely. These chemicals work like medicine we take into our own bodies. If a person consumes an overdose, he or she commits suicide. In that same manner, if too much chemical is used on a pond, it will eradicate the weeds, but it will have also eradicated the fish as well. It is also very important to improve and to restore the bottom of the ponds. If we have to maintain the bottom of the pond, we must empty the fish pond. At times we have to leave the soil uncultivated or combine treatment with a crop. The bottom of the pond could be broken superficially by plowing more or less deeply, dredge out the silted matter from the bottom which causes swampy vegetation to germinate. When fish ponds are maintained properly, it will increase fish productivity.

3. Liming and Fertilizing of the Pond: The use of lime in a pond increases the production of ponds. Lime has variable action, but it is favorable to both the hygienic condition of both the pond and the fish there in.

Liming is important in ponds where there is shortage of calcium. In waters where there is less than 10 ppm total hardness, the addition of lime will increase the production of fish. Lime affects the bottom mud where it changes colloidal properties and creates an alkaline environment which is more suitable for bacteria and fungi (Bennett, 1971). Lime increases the rate of decay. It also has chemical actions such as the precipitation of iron compounds. It will also prevent the poisonous properties of sodium, potassium and magnesium ions.

In soft water, the addition of lime may be followed by an increase in carbon dioxide storage in the form of bicarbonate (Huet, 1986; Bennett, 1971).

Swingle believes that calcium competes with the algae for the carbon dioxide. Nielson on the other hand believes that aquatic plants use bicarbonate directly in photo synthesis, up to one-half of the amount present in water. Thus both Bennett (1971) and Huet (1986) believe that the addition of lime on the pond floor will increase the production of fish in the pond.

Huet believes that manuring or fertilizing improves and accelerates the production of natural food in the ponds. From this fact, stocking and production are greatly improved to over 50%, when compared with the natural production of non-fertilized ponds.

4. Feeding Fish in Ponds: Feeding fish in ponds or distributing artificial food is one of the major means of increasing production in fish cultivation. Feed efficiency is usually expressed in one of the two ways:

$$\text{Feed Conversion Ratio} = \frac{\text{feed intake}}{\text{weight gain}}$$

$$\text{or Conversion Efficiency} = \frac{\text{weight gain}}{\text{feed intake}} \times 100$$

These are expressed as ratios of dry weight of feed to net weight of the animal. The rapidly growing fry of 0.25 g require as much as 10% of their weight daily, but when they grow to reach to about 4 grams, then the ratio of feed can be reduced to about 5% of their body weight daily.

According to Pillay (1993), most farmers over feed their fish at the fry stage for better growth and survival. The frequency of feeding decreases from eight times a day for fry

A Sheltered fjord in Norway, used for Cage Fish Farming

There are usually accumulations of un used feeds.

This leads to oxygen demand and toxic gases.

Pond farm in swampy area. Most suitable for Carp, Tilapia, and

Cartfish in fresh waters. In such farms , dike design and

weighing 1.5 grams to four times a day for advanced fry. Fish farmers keep a daily chart to guide in daily feeding in grow-out farms. It is believed that feeding in excess of twice a day has no beneficial effect on growth rate or food conversion efficiency (Pillay, 1993).

The feeding ratio has to be adjusted according to the water temperature which affects the metabolic rate of the animals. Many culturists do not feed in winter, and below 7° C, the fish may not consume much feed, except on warmer days. In Africa, for that matter, the feeding should be done daily as it is always hot. The temperatures in Africa are generally above 40° F except in few places in southern Africa every day of the year.

5. Fish Production in Ponds: Fish production in ponds can also be increased by biological means, such as a careful choice of species. If fish production is to be increased then species for stocking should be selected very carefully. It is very necessary to choose the type of species that are fitted for that particular region. In Africa, fish to be stocked should be suitable for high water temperatures. As all informed farmers know that different species grow in different regions. It is important to select species that will do well in the location where the farmer is. *Tilapia* species are the ones that can be cultivated in various locations of the African continent. A mixture of two *Tilapia* species would be more profitable. One of the *Tilapia* species should be herbivorous and the other microphagous-omnivorous. In certain African countries, *carp* and *Heterotis niloticus* are raised with success. If the various species suitable for Africa are carefully selected, then fish production in Africa will increase to a certain degree.

6. Controlling the Stocking of Ponds: The stocking depends on productivity and the size of the pond. The total amount of fish should be dependent at least on the productivity due to fertilization and artificial feeding. Most of these have been discussed in this chapter. As we have stated before, that fertilizer increases the presence of the plants in the ponds. The fertilizers help to increase the plants in the water body. These plants act as food for fish in the pond. The more one fertilizes, the more fish will be produced because there will be plenty of food for fish. It is also important to realize that excessive fertilization will result into excessive plant life in the pond which will consume all the oxygen in the pond which the fish in the water need. Thus, it is necessary that fertilization should be just enough which will result into just enough plant life in the pond.

Temperature is also important for the productivity of fish in ponds. The warmer the ponds, the more the fish will be produced. Since Africa is generally warm, the water temperature on the farmers' ponds in Africa is certain and therefore fish production will also be increased.

The deeper the pond, the more the space for fish in the pond. In some parts of Africa, it gets pretty hot and the water in the pond reduces. If the pond is shallow, the fish will not have anywhere to hide. But if the ponds are deeper there will be many places for fish to hide even if some water reduces. When the ponds are too deep, the deeper parts will not experience as much heat as the shallow waters. Thus ponds should be as deep as will be necessary to maintain the necessary heat, but also to allow enough space for fish to play. Thus, controlling the stocking in the pond and also maintaining the necessary temperature will promote fish production.

7. Integrated Fish Farming: Production of fish and production of vegetation nearby will increase the quantity and quality of fish in ponds. The rearing of fish and ducks together will also increase the fish yield. The duck's droppings will be regularly spread over the ponds. This will provide organic manure in the pond and also at the bottom of the pond. This will result in production of plankton and algae by which *Tilapia* and other species of fish will be fed. Thus, duck droppings will replace other manures or even to supplement it.

Ducks, as we all know, are water birds. They are usually fed while floating on surface of the ponds. The droppings or the food that drops at the bottom which is not utilized will result in an indirect manure. Ducks have shown to fight fish disease that would destroy the fish stock or even endanger human beings too, such as bilharzia. Such programs has been practiced in Zambia.

The combination of fish and poultry is an excellent way to promote agriculture particularly in the form of fish farming (Huet, 1986). Rice-fish cultivation is important everywhere in the Far East and in some parts of Europe. In Africa, Madagascar is probably the most famous for this integrated system of aquaculture.

8. Intermediate Fishing: Intermediate fishing is necessary when the density of the population of fish is too great. Sometimes too much production of fish in pond will spoil the stock, therefore to reduce the fish population in pond will improve the quality of fish in the pond. But when the population is too dense, the fish do not have enough space and the food eventually will become inadequate.

Intermediate can only be done when the population is too dense. This might have resulted from the very beginning when the original stock was planted. Too many fish might have been stocked in the pond or it might have been the specie in the pond which reproduces too profusely such as *Tilapia*. In the original stocking whereby too many fish were put in the pond results into many species of unequal growth. There may be two types of species, one of which is not spawning. In this case, intermediate fishing will remove the mature fish of the specie that is spawning and reproducing. The smaller fish will be left in the pond to increase in size.

In the second case where the specie in the pond reproduces too much such as *Tilapia*, some bigger fish should be removed and leave smaller ones in the pond. Sometimes the smaller fish which will be left will spawn and reproduce too much, so to reduce this type of population, intermediate fishing can be used to also include some of the small fish, so as to cut down the number in the pond. Too much population leads to inadequate food in the pond or oxygen will be consumed faster than it ought to be. Intermediate fishing can be carried out using lines, trap nets, seize nets, cast nets, or bamboo lattice. In Africa, Madagascar and in many other parts such as Uganda, Zambia, Zimbabwe, South Africa, this intermediate fishing is utilized to reduce the dense fish population.

9. Control of Diseases: If fish farming is to succeed in any country, the fish farmers must ensure that the fish they are producing are healthy. The fish that are imported from outside should not be allowed in the country without serious scrutiny. Diseases are usually brought in the country through live fish. Some countries may import fingerlings from other outside country, but before any contract is signed, the people responsible must make sure that these young fish (fingerlings) do not come from diseased locations. These fingerlings should be scrutinized to make sure the disease do not come in to spread to other healthy locations in your nation. If careful attention is paid by the farmers to make sure no diseased fish are brought in the country and if all fish in the country are examined from time to time to ensure health fish are being produced, certainly fish farming production will be increased. This subject of "disease control" will be discussed further in later chapter.

As we discussed, the issues and methods of increasing fish farming production in Africa, we should bear in mind that fish farming will never develop unless the producers are trained. Many fish farmers are ignorant of this subject of fish farming. Many fish farmers choose to be fish farmers without seriously weighing pros and cons of this endeavor. Fish farming is a scientific occupation, which by all means must be scientifically carried out. Although the farmers in Africa are not scientifically oriented individuals, but with the training, advice, and assistance by the extension officers, they should be able to acquire enough information to enable them to carry out this profession without too many problems.

Training of Fish Farmers

Since fish farming in Africa was imported from outside the continent, the project planners should train farmers in various areas. This will improve fish farming performance among farmers. Farmers need to know some information about fish farming, if fish farming is going to improve its production. There are many areas in which fish farmers need information, namely:

Pond Site Selection: Site selection is one of the important points a farmer needs to know. Extension agents need to help farmers in selecting sites where to place the fish ponds. The farmers should have in mind the plans they have for their land. Once a pond is placed there, it will destroy all other plans for those locations permanently. Even if the farmer changes his or her mind from fish farming, the pond will still be there. It is all the more important to know how to make good decisions for selecting places where fish ponds should be located (Pillay, 1993). The size of the pond will depend on a number of factors such as the quantity of water, the extent of land, the technology to be used. The technology can be classified as extensive, semi-intensive, or intensive farming. The farmers must also know that their ponds are in locations which are appropriate where droughts will not dry out the water from the ponds, or where too much rain will not flood out the place so as to destroy the ponds. The location should be in such a way that the enterprise will be economically viable, and accessibility to markets will be possible. All these factors are to be considered by the farmers if the locations are to be appropriately used in increasing fish farming production (Pillay, 1993).

Water Supply: Fish farmers need to consider the type of water supply available. Is the water surface run-off, underground seepage, or a flowing spring? These points may be difficult for a farmer to know by himself or herself, the type of water available. The extension worker needs to come out strong in assisting the farmer in making these decisions. Farmers need to be taught how to recognize the run-off water in comparison to the spring water. Unless decisions are made based on the right information and understanding, the farmer may run a risk of finding the pond dry during the dry seasons (Pillay, 1993).

The size of the pond will depend on the amount of water available. It is vital to estimate the flow before planing the pond. This information may be acquired more appropriately if the extension worker also offers to help. A flowing spring is usually the best source of water for a pond. When constructing a pond, farmers should be taught to think of the downstream neighbors. If there are neighbors who might be affected by the pond, they might bring legal action to prevent the pond construction. Thus, the extension workers should assist farmers to think along these lines before the ponds are started (Huet, 1986).

By considering the amount, the source, the type and the minerals in the water, will assist greatly the farmer in his fish farming production.

Soils: In course of informal training of the farmers, the extension worker should bring under consideration the effects of soils. The soil texture characteristics that might affect fish pond construction are ground water level, stoniness, depth to bedrock, soil stability, soil strength, compaction, shrink-swell potential, organic matter content, and rate of permeability. Usually fish ponds are dug, taking in consideration, the ground water level. If the ground water level is too deep, this might require a very deep pond to reach this ground water level. The extension of stoniness or bedrock close to the surface makes it difficult to construct any type of a pond. Pond construction needs stable, strong soil. Dug out ponds cannot be constructed in water bearing sand that flow when uncovered. Not many farmers can have this type of information by themselves. Extension workers should be of great help to teach farmers some of these things which are vital to their fish pond construction (Huet, 1986).

Size: When helping farmers to know more about fish cultivation, the extension workers need to discuss the size of each pond. Warm water fish ponds should at least be one acre in size (Huet, 1986).

Shoreline: A vegetative cover should be established on the banks of the pond to prevent erosion. Some ponds may need rock-rap on the shoreline to prevent wave action or to control burrowing animals. Plants that grow in the water along the shore are not desirable in a farm of fish ponds. Since most plants do not grow in water, three feet deep nd steep

Injecting Patuirary homogenates to induce spawning.
This is done in Fish Farms where controlled breeding
is practised.

Pond Farm in Zambia, one of the biggest in Subsaharan Africa.

Contour type of pond farm.

slopes on the shoreline will help prevent most aquatic animals from coming into the pond

(Huet, 1986).

Management: In helping farmers to learn about fish cultivation, they need to be

informed that a successful fish pond must be managed (Pillay, 1993). If one is not willing to

take time and effort to manage the pond, chances of having a successful pond are slim.

It must also be understood that farmers need to keep a pond diary to record specific

stocking, weed treatment, fish removal and angling. This will be a viable reference in

knowing what kinds and how many to stock in the future, what type of weed treatment to use

and how successful the pond is producing and what is really wanted (Pillay, 1993).

Types of Ponds

Farmers need to be helped to know the various types of ponds so that they can make

wise choices of a pond which fit the available conditions. Ponds can be divided into:

1. Spring water ponds: This is the type whose water comes from the bottom of the

pond or in close proximity to it supplied by ground water.

2. Ponds supplied by rainwater or run-off water: After draining this pond dry,

this pond fills up more or less quickly, according to its size, and to the amount of water or

rainfall.

3. Ponds supplied by a water course: These are classified as (a) barrage ponds and

(b) diversion ponds according to whether all the water course or only part crosses the ponds.

Diversion ponds are sometimes subdivided into (a) linked ponds and (b) parallel ponds. In

both cases, the by-pass channel evaluates unnecessary and access water. From these types of ponds, the farmers can choose the type of pond that will be suitable to the conditions available in his area (Huet, 1986; Pillay, 1993).

Fish Pond Monitoring

As extension agent helps farmers learn more about fish cultivation, it is vital that fish pond management is discussed. In fish cultivation, monitoring involves surveying various conditions. The fish are sensitive to changes in temperature, oxygen, pH alkaline and water. The farmer should be aware and should always be monitoring and assessing these elements. If fish are swimming near the surface, the water needs to be circulated to increase oxygen levels (Chakroff, 1981). If possible, monitoring of ponds should be rotated to spread the work evenly.

Monitoring can also be used as means of evaluation. If there are problems within the pond, ongoing evaluation should be in place to detect the changes that take place. If for example, large quantities of fish died due to malnutrition, the feeding methods must be changed immediately. The farmers owning these ponds must participate in this phase of the project. Their satisfaction, disappointments and suggestions should be taken seriously so that changes can be made in the project. Evaluation should be made of quantitative and qualitative data, and the criteria be developed by farmers, extension staff and the researchers. It is difficult to measure success rates. With fish farming, it is not easy to gauge input, especially labor, but estimations can be made in respect to changes (Chakroff, 1981).

<u>Training Procedures</u>

In the initial discussions with the farmers, the extension agent should find out the farmer's needs and objectives for investing in fish cultivation.

<u>Needs Assessment</u>

A checklist of needs assessments can help in reviewing the assumptions. It is possible to assume that farmers are poor and ignorant of fish cultivation, but after studying their needs assessment, one can change his or her views regarding their abilities. Thus the extension agent's approach in helping them learn about fish culture will depend on their articulated views.

Before the actual meeting, the extension agent should plan for it. He should know the number of farmers who are expected to attend. He will then plan for the place of meeting, the material needed, and the agenda for that meeting. If the number will be big, then the place will be in such a way as to accommodate people in small groups if this will be needed. The material should be many enough so that every farmer that will come will be served without difficulty (Knox, 1986).

Those farmers should be informed in writing of the procedures to be followed in advance. This will help the planner and the visiting farmers from embarrassment. At the actual time of the meeting, the agent needs to follow the procedures as they are outlined in the information letter so that confusion is avoided.

When the meeting opens, farmers will want information to be prepared for them, regarding fish culture project. If the program meets the farmers' needs, this might encourage them to persist and even try to practice what they are learning. If fish cultivation meets the farmers' immediate needs such as provision of food for their immediate families, generation of income to help them meet the necessities of life, the farmers will be willing to get involved in such a venture.

In soliciting needs assessment from farmers, the extension agent may want to conduct discussions. It is not good to conduct lectures to these farmers, but rather discussing with them would be more appropriate. Extension agent needs to ask questions that will extract information regarding their indigenous knowledge. It would be more appropriate to find out the farmer's current proficiency regarding fish cultivation and the type of fish they have in the location. These people may not have as much information as the extension agent has, but it should not be taken for granted that they know nothing. It is on this indigenous knowledge that the extension agent will add his expert knowledge (Compton, 1993).

It is important to learn that local farmers would appreciate much to see their local knowledge being used than seeing new knowledge from abroad. They would appreciate much to see local resources developed than to see transfer technology from outside. It is therefore very important for farmers to be given an opportunity to assess their own needs. This will encourage and even provide insights to farmers regarding their own abilities or weaknesses, which will motivate them to engage in learning more about fish cultivation to meet their needs.

Required Proficiency

In the course of discussion with farmers, the extension agent will discover the farmer's current proficiency. It will then be possible to realize their discrepancies between current proficiency and the required proficiency regarding fish cultivation. This will help the extension agent and the farmers to set up study goals that will enhance their knowledge level to the requisite proficiency (Knox, 1987). When farmers go back and after realization of their proficiency will assist them in their self-directed learning efforts, through reading literature written about fish cultivation, or through visiting other farmers who might be engaged in the same business.

In some cases, some farmers may know nothing about fish cultivation, then the extension agent will have to work with them in acquiring these proficiencies. In this case also self-directed learning can supplement supervised learning activities. Videos, films, and slides prepared mainly on local fish cultivation will help these farmers in their efforts (Knox, 1987).

In working with these farmers, the extension agent should be interested in their development as they move from one stage to another. The farmer's proficiency will develop from being dependent on other people's advice to being independent in doing the business themselves.

These farmers, just like other adults, will have different learning styles. Their learning styles will depend on intelligence, personality, age, their formal education and previous experience in fish culture (Knox, 1986). All these will contribute to their fast development from one stage to the next. These farmers will also learn faster and participate more if they have big problems in their homes, such as big debts which fish cultivation may help to alleviate, or the depletion of soil in which case fish culture will help replace those other crops or loss of a job which may be replaced by fish cultivation.

Extension agent needs to discover the farmers' learning styles and use those to individualize their learning. This can be done through asking for their preferences. Those will assist the extension agent to decide on the instructional materials (Knox, 1986). The extension agent and the farmers will select the styles that fit the situations. Teaching in this case will mean helping farmers to acquire deeper knowledge about issues related to fish cultivation.

Question Methods

In training small scale farmers we need to use local facilities. Many farmers can be invited in a community hall, a room in a local school, a church basement, one resident's home, etc. Farmers do not need to be restricted to any particular locations when extension agent plans to train them in fish culture. They can even sit down under a tree and discuss.

In conducting these discussions, question method will be most appropriate. The extension agent should make sure that the farmers feel enough rapport and familiarity with him and among themselves that they are prepared to interact and deal with the questions. He should encourage all farmers to participate by giving equal opportunities to speak to as many people as possible. He should study the subject to be covered very carefully and prepare questions which will extract information to exhaust the subject at issue. He should follow the participants' trend of thinking and use the questions to help them progress. Sometimes questions may have to deal with assumptions, influences, facts and interpretations, relationships, reasons, procedures, application or implications. This will necessitate learning

well the content and the learning farmers (Knox, 1986). The extension agent can use

questions to broaden discussions with farmers and also explore their varying viewpoints and

to keep the discussions on the track. He can also use questions to create interest and sharing

among the farmers. The agent should be very good at asking questions and give time to

farmers to think about them before they can respond. Careful listening should be encouraged.

The extension agent needs to prepare the materials to be discussed. He should list discussable

issues or problems for that session. This will encourage farmers to keep coming as they feel

that their time is not being wasted (Knox, 1987).

CHAPTER IV

FISH FARMING IN VARIOUS NATIONS OF AFRICA

In view that fish farming in Africa is still new, the development plan of this farming system should include long-term financial and marketing assistance. The target group is subsistence farmers but focusing on commercialization of aquaculture rather than family nutrition as the overall objective.

Although fish farming has been in existence for a long time in Africa, its development has only begun in recent years. Since 1924 when fish farming was first emphasized in Kenya for domestic family nutrition, now after 72 years, fish farming has increased about ten times. The table below shows how much each region of the world contributes to the world fish farming production.

Fish culture production in various regions of the world.

Region	Finfish (MT+%)	Molluscs (MT+%)	Crustaceans	Total
Asia and Oceania	2,912,150 (72.7%)	4,466,150 (84.4%)	133,550 (79.1%)	7,511,850 (79.3%)
Latin America	21,500 (0.5%)	38,500 (0.7%)	17,900 (10.6%)	77,900 (0.8%)
Africa	11,550 (0.3%)	250 (0.0%)	- -	11,800 (0.1%)
North America	154,950 (3.9%)	144,800 (0.7%)	17,450 (10.3%)	317,200 (3.3%)
Europe	908,150 (22.6%)	643,900 (12.2%	100 (0.0%)	1,552,150 (16.5%)
TOTAL	4,008,300 (42.3%)	5,293,600 (55.9%)	169,000 (1.8%)	9,470,900 (100.0%)

Source: Huisman, 1986.

MAP SHOWING FISH FARMING NATIONS OF AFRICA

When one examines the table carefully, one finds that Asia and the Islands in the Pacific Ocean produce the biggest amount of fish in the world. They produce 79.3%. Europe follows Asia; they produce 16.5%. Then North America is third with 3.3%, Latin America with 0.8%, and Africa comes last and we produce 0.1%. One can see that Africa's fish farming is basically for subsistence. It is important that the picture be changed from subsistence fish farming to commercial fish culture. I believe this can be done. It is important at this juncture to discuss fish farming in various selected countries of Africa. This will give the reader a picture of what goes on in Africa in respect to fish farming.

THE ARAB REPUBLIC OF EGYPT

The total water area in Egypt of aquaculture is about 2,500 ha. But more than 300,000 hectares can be used for fish farming. Systems such as monoculture, polyculture of exotic and indigenous species are practiced. Finfish fry are received either naturally or by pond breeding. Up to about 2.25-3.25 metric tons are produced every year. The major problems affecting fish farming in Egypt are the great demand for fish fry and the need for the great amount of supplementary feed which would be utilized in helping fish in ponds to spawn profusely.

Although in Egypt today the total fish production is about 105,000 tons, the great demand for fish in Egypt is increasing because of the increasing population in the country. Because of this great demand for fish food due to the increasing population, fish farming practices have progressed fast in the last few years.

Mirror Carp was introduced in Egypt in 1970; mainly for the improvement of the species which were grown in Egypt since 1949. Aquaculture is not new in Egypt, as it was practiced in ancient times. Fish farming was practiced in the country as far back as 2500 B.C. But the scientific approach to fish farming in Egypt started in 1934. At present fish farming production in Egypt is still low and underdeveloped. Economically, aquaculture contributes very little to the economy of the country.

Status of Fish Farming

Fish farming in Egypt is practiced in fresh, brackish, and saltwater everywhere in the country. The total area under fish farming use is about 2500 ha. But experimental and commercial fish farming are being conducted mainly on the government farms. Some private farms also run commercial fish farming. Inside the country, ponds, reservoirs, dams, tanks are stocked with fry and used as farms for open fish farming.

Fish farming in Egypt is done by individual people on their own farms. The family man owning the ponds manages them with the help of his family members. Some more people are hired to join the work during harvest time.

Species Cultivated: The mirror carp, *Cyprinus carpio v. specularis* is now the principal specie produced in Egypt. Of the indigenous species, *Tilapia nilotica, T. zillii, T. galilea, Mugil cephalus, M. Capito, M. Saliens, M. chello, Clarias lazera, Anguilla valgaris, Solea vulgaris, Chrysophris (sparus), aurata, Dicentrarchus labrax, Morone panctata.* Many types of exotic species have been introduced to Egypt between 1934-1970. In 1934, the common carp, *Cyprinus carpio v. communis* was introduced from Indonesia. Fry were stocked in the Nile and in all other smaller rivers and tributaries, and they had no effect in these waters. They were replaced by the mirror carp *Cyprinus carpio v. specularis* were introduced from France, the black bass *Micropterus salmoides* and *Tilapia massambica* from Thailand in 1954. These species spawned well and achieved good growth.

The silver carps (*Hypophthalmichthys molitrix*) and the grass carp (*Ctenopharyngodon idella* were introduced from Japan in 1962 and from Hong Kong in 1968. The two species did well in the Egyptian waters.

In 1970 a new type of *mirror carp*, which resembled the *German carp*, was introduced to Egypt for the purpose of improving fish species which had been used in the country since 1949 (Bolock, 1972).

Fish Farms in Egypt

1. Barrage Farm: This is a freshwater fish farm which was started in 1929 at El Kanatira El Khairia. The farm consists of 25 spawning, nursing and experimental ponds. All fish species which are brought in Egypt go through this farm for acclimatization and spawning. The indigenous species of *Clarias lazera*, and other experiment on induced breeding are conducted here on this farm.

2. Another fish farm known as El Serow Farm was established in 1949. It has 67 earthen ponds, with a total area of 16 hectares. It is a private farm which produces *carp fish* fry.

3. El Max Experimental Fish Farm: This farm collects and produces *mullet* and *eel* fry from the sea. The brackish and marine water species are experimented upon on this farm. It was established in 1931 near Alexandria and it has 13 ponds.

4. There are many private farms all over the country. But each of these farms depend on these fish fry producing farms for their fingerlings, mono, and polyculture with feeding and fertilization are conducted on these fry producing farms.

Fish Farming Systems Used in Egypt

(a) There are many irrigation canals and drainage systems which have water all year. The water in these canals, drainage systems and River Nile is suitable for cage fish farming. *Carps* and *clarias* are kept in cages which are suspended from wooden boards across the canals.

(b) Lakes and reservoirs are another system of fish farming in Egypt. Lake Quarun is an isolated and closed lake. It is situated 83 miles south of the city of Cairo. There is too much evaporation in these regions of Egypt and as such water sometimes dries up in those lakes and reservoirs. This increases the amount of salinity to about 29 ppt. This led to the diminishing of lake fish productions. *Tilapia zillii* continue to flourish on the mouth of these rivers.

Fish fry such as mullets (*Mugil caphalus, M. capito, M. saliens, M. chello* and *M. seheli*), *Solea vulgaris*, and *Chrysophris*, (*sparus*), *aurata*, were transplanted from 1928-1970. *Solea vulgaris* spawned and reproduced very successfully in new environments. Plans to transplant other species such as *Dicentrarchus labrax* and *Morone punctata* along with the shrimp is very much underworld.

Natural Sources of Fry

Egypt is a great producer of fry. Sometimes fish fry are found on the mouth of a river and many fish fry are collected. Some are sent to individual farmers, but some are taken to fish fry producing centers. As much as 20 million mullets and eel fry are collected annually, from El Max Center alone.

Some of these fry are stocked in cement ponds, where fertilized eggs are received on special egg receptacles. These fry are sent to the hatching and nursing ponds. In about 3-4 weeks, the produced fry 3-5 cm, are ready for stocking. *Clarias lazera* are produced in the same way, however, artificial food are offered to *Clarias* fry to prevent predation.

Some fry are obtained by induced breeding. *Chinese carp* (*silver* and *grass carp*) has been partially successful in Egypt. Laboratory for induced breeding of mullets and *Chrysophris, (sparus), aurata* is almost reaching completion in Egypt at Lake Quarun (Bolock, 1972).

Cultural Practices in Egypt:

(1) Organized culture in man made ponds. In this system, controlled mono and polyculture of *carps, Tilapia, mullets*, and *clarias* are practiced. Supplementary food is usually given. About 2.25 tons hectares of market-size carp are produced in monoculture, the rearing period is about 8 months. The supplementary food such as cotton-seed cakes and rice

bran are offered. The percentage loss varies from 8-50 percent depending whether there is the presence of *Clarias lazera* which is a carnivorous fish.

(2) <u>Transformation of illegal enclosures to organized farms</u>. Some parts of delta lakes are illegally enclosed with earth dikes and fished illegally many times a year. These are harmful to lake fisheries. These enclosures are turned into legal fish farms where polyculture of *carps, mullets, tilapia* and *clarias* is done with supplementary feeding.

(3) <u>Rehabilitation of old ponds</u>. Almost in every province in Egypt one can find old ponds which can be rehabilitated and are stocked with *mullets, carps* and *Tilapia* fry. Supplementary feeding is practiced. The ponds are then fished after 8-10 months of rearing.

(4) <u>Fish farming in rice-fields</u>. Fish farming in rice-fields was first done in Egypt in 1954. After rearing *carp* fingerlings for 2-3 months a total production of about 200 kg per hectare was achieved. The production of rice also increased by about 5-7 percent. In Egypt there are 300,000 hectares of cultivated rice-fields. If all these hectares were stocked with fish fry, there would be more than 30,000 metric tons of fish produced. This has not been tried.

<u>Problems Affecting Fish Farming in Egypt</u>

About 400,000 hectares of fresh, brackish, and saltwater areas can be turned into fish farms. These locations are so fertile that with addition of supplementary feeding, good production could easily be achieved. There are some problems which must be overcome before successful fish farming can be conducted:

(1) There is great need of supplementary food for cultivated fish. Cotton seed cakes and rice bran which are used as food for fish are also used to fatten cattle. The available quantity is not enough for both cattle and fish.

(2) There is a shortage of fish fry such as *carp, Tilapia, clarias* and whatever is available is not even enough for the present fish farms. One fish fry producing center is needed in each county.

(3) Big induced breeding laboratory is needed where fry from the brackish and marine water fish are in demand.

(4) It is difficult to transmit fish farming knowledge to all fish farmers in the country. Some still want to remain hidden so that they are not taxable and others in remote places where fish farming agents may not get to them (Kaura R. and A.R. El Bolock, 1972).

THE REPUBLIC OF SUDAN

In 1950, a committee on fisheries agreed to write to the colonial office regarding starting fish farming in Sudan. In 1951, Dr. Hickling drafted a five-point plan in which he suggested that 100 feddans or 42 hectares be used for fisheries project in Sudan. If this project could be successful, then the project could be expanded. He suggested also that eight 4 acre ponds be used. He ordered that research and development should be kept independent of each other.

Dr. C. F. Hickling's objective was to try fish production on an experimental basis. If this pilot project succeeded, then fish farming could be included in the agricultural sector of the country.

The Fisheries Standing Committee decided to start a fish farm at Gordan's Tree which was later called Shagarra Farm. This committee decided that fish farming could be successful in the northern part of the country. In this region aquaculture would be mixed in the agricultural economy (George, 1969).

Fish Farm at Shagarra

The Standing Fisheries Committee started a fisheries farm at Shagarra. It was a demonstration center, where various farmers could come and learn about fish farming. This farm was six miles south of Khartoum on the White Nile. This was one of the fish farms of the Sudan Government's Five-year Development Budget Plans (1951-1956). They desired to study the authochthonus and other species (Anon, 1955).

In the Second Government's Five-year Budget Plan of 1956-1961, the Shagarra Farm project was ordered to be closed down. The original objective of the farm was to find out whether fish farming was viable in Sudan. But this was not carried out as intended. The government decided to emphasize the "Inland Fisheries Research."

This institute expanded into 60 hectare earthen ponds farm--comprising of 37 ponds.

(i)   There were spawning ponds - 4 ponds.

(ii) Nursery ponds - 12 ponds.

(iii) Rearing ponds - 6 ponds.

(iv) Growing ponds - 7 ponds.

There was a total of 37 ponds altogether. These were managed by one fisheries officer, with one technologist, four fishermen, and five laborers. There was a small laboratory equipped with a few biological and limnological studies (Anon, 1958).

Species of Cultured Fish

According to Pekkola, 1918, there were three indigenous species which belonged to *Tilapia*. These were *T. nilotica, T. galilaea*, and *T. zillii*. The most desirable of the three was the *T. nilotica*, and other species were *Lates niloticus, Labeo niloticus* and *Clarias vulgaris*.

Exotic Species

In 1974 exotic specie called *Gambusia affinis* was introduced to Shagarra. This specie was brought to Sudan from Italy. *Tilapia melanopleura* was introduced in Gezira Canal. The purpose for this specie was to control weeds and bilharzia in canals and rivers. This species, however, was found to be eating diatoms and could not eat flowering plants. It could not feed on *potamogeton nodosus*. This species of *Tilapia melanopleura* could not be used to control weeds as was expected.

Fish culture mission to Sudan in 1972 suggested that *T. melanopleura* be associated with *T. nilotica* to give an additional amount of production. But all *Tilapia* species breed too freely, and when the two species of *Tilapia* combine there will be even greater production (Huet, 1959).

In the 'haffirs,' pond fertilization and artificial feeding cannot be used. The water in these rivers and canals which lead to River Nile is meant for drinking and therefore no fertilizers and food left overs could be put in the water. Because of this, George in 1974 recommended the introduction of Chinese grass carp, because it feeds on weeds which could easily be supplied. Grass carps can be controlled, as it cannot reproduce in confined waters without hypophysation. In 1975, the Government of India presented the Government of Sudan with 10,000 common grass carp and these were acclimatized in these exotic species in Sudanese pond waters.

Other Species

Hofstede (1955-1956) and Huet (1959) observed that *T. nilotica* produced, but almost uncared for. There was no pond fertilization and there was no artificial feeding. In such conditions it was difficult to produce fish of marketable size. When *Lates niloticus, T. nilotica* showed good growth, mainly because the population was controlled by *Lates niloticus* eating some of the fish in the pond. In 1956-1957, Hofstede mentioned a good animal yield which was 394 kg in 18 months from the four acres ponds. There were species such as *Alestes, Labeo, Lates niloticus, Hydrocyon, Synodontis, Auchanoglanis, Tetradon, Cicharinus,* and *Distichodus*. All these species were produced in ponds in Sudan in 1955-1959.

Further study was conducted regarding artificial feeding, the use of organic and inorganic fertilizers. It was observed that broad beans are suitable as feed for *T. nilotica*. With a combination of superphosphate and poultry manure, increased the production of fish in ponds, canals, reservoirs and dams.

Hofstede in 1958 found out that *Labeo sp.* reach maturity at a length of 35 cm. At this time the male fish deliver milt with pressure on belly, and the female are full of eggs. From April to September female fish breed three to four times at the bottom of 75 cm and after spawning, females grow more slowly than males.

Comparative studies on the exotic mosquito fish, *Gambusia affinis* and *T. nilotica* as larvivores are in progress (George, 1975). More work on acclimatization and compatibility of the other exotic species, *C. carpio* and *C. idella* are still going on. The experimental work is restricted to Shagarra Fish Farm. Great caution is to be taken regarding the introduction of exotic species in these rivers and canals, for fear that these species could upset the biological balance of the indigenous fisheries on chance entry into the Nile. As a result a Fish Culture Research Camp for Training and production was set up at Shagarra in January 1975. This was to make a closer study of these exotic species.

In November 1957, El Ain Reservoir was stocked with 15 cm *Tilapia nilotica*. In 1959 Golo and Mellit Reservoirs were stocked with 12-15 cm *T. nilotica*. In the Andi Region with heavy rainfall, many barrage ponds were constructed. George in 1959 made a survey of the Miri Bara Dam and recommended the introduction of polyculture, including *T. nilotica, Labeo niloticus* and others. Mixed farming is being encouraged in the regions of Khartoum province, Hasas-Heisa and Wad Medani.

The extension services, under the Fisheries and Hydrobiological Administration Section, selects the site for ponds, provides construction specifications, and free *T. nilotica* fingerling for stocking. In 1974, nursery, rearing and growing ponds were constructed in Baboud's Farm. All ponds that were constructed were big growing ponds.

The nursery, rearing, and growing ponds should be encouraged throughout Sudan. The information about the status of fish culture in the reservoirs, and private farms is inadequate. The biggest problem is the shortages of trained and experienced officers. Statistical information must be provided to the researcher, for planning future research programs.

THE REPUBLIC OF UGANDA

Fish farming started in Uganda in 1931. It was in this year that *Oreochromis S. niger* was transferred from Kenya to Lake Bunyonyi in Uganda (Balarin, 1985). In 1935, *Oreochromis niloticus* were distributed to various lakes such as Victoria, Kyoga, and Albert. *Oreochromis leucosticus* and *Tilapia zillii* were distributed in 1951. In this period also *trout* and *black bass* were introduced into high altitude Uganda streams (FAO, 1985). Between 1931 and 1943, fish farming was done in lakes and rivers by foreign experts who were basically British and a few other expatriates from France, Germany and Italy. These expert individuals used mainly exotic species as they had no knowledge of indigenous ones.

It was in 1953 that the first ponds were started in Uganda. They were not dug by individual farmers. They were constructed by Game and Fisheries Department at Kajansi Experimental Station (Balarin, 1985). Kajansi Experimental Station was started as a demonstration center for fish farming in Uganda. By 1954, the Center was fully operational. The Center has classrooms and laboratories that were established at the site to learn more about the indigenous species.

UGANDA - SHOWING DISTRICT BOUNDARIES

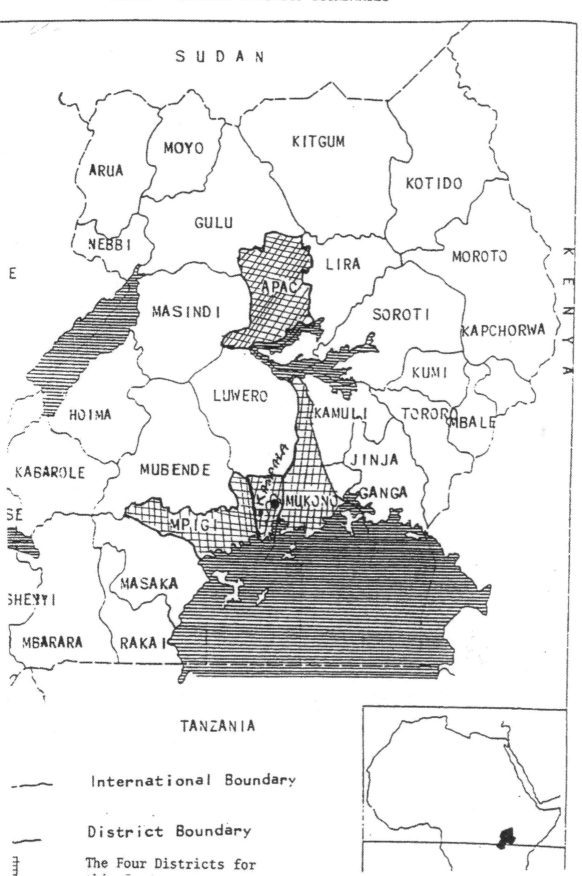

SUDAN

ARUA

MOYO

KITGUM

KOTIDO

GULU

NEBBI

MASINDI

LIRA

APAC

MOROTO

SOROTI

KAPCHORWA

KUMI

LUWERO

KAMULI

TORORO

MBALE

HOIMA

KABAROLE

MUBENDE

JINJA

GANGA

MUKONO

MPIGI

MASAKA

SHEYYI

MBARARA

RAKAI

KENYA

TANZANIA

International Boundary

District Boundary

The Four Districts for

Fish ponds by individual farmers were started in Kasese in 1952. These ponds were around Kilemba mines. Four ponds belonged to Yofesi Masereka, Daudi Kitesoboire, and William Kule. The four ponds were well stocked and the fish were healthy as they swam and fed well. Kilembe mines administration desired to destroy them, because they wanted to expand their mining locations. Mr. S. N. Semakula, the Regional Fisheries officer, at Lake Katwe, mentioned in a letter he wrote to these three people, above, that any pond that was constructed after 1953 could not be compensated. It is possible that the owners of these ponds claimed that these ponds were dug in 1952, so that they could get compensation (Uganda Government Files No. 1/2 Fisheries Department, 1993).

Although fish farming was slow at the beginning, by 1959 there were 5000 ponds in various locations in Uganda (FAO, 1984). Between 1962 and 1966, nearly 90% of fish pond activities were concentrated in Kyadondo, Bulemezi, Singo and Busiro Counties. There were fish ponds in other districts such as Kabale in Kigezi, Mbale in Bugishu, Busenyi in Ankole district, Toro, Gulu, West Nile, and Kotido in the dry northeast of Uganda. The first ponds were of all shapes and sizes, but were mainly built at the edge of swamps, rivers, and springs. A few of these relied on rainfall for their water supply. At times some of these ponds dried up due to prolonged drought (FAO, 1985).

In 1962-1966, Mr. Pruginin, the officer in charge at Kajansi Experimental Station started doing research on *carp culture, Tilapia hybridization* and predator control (Balarin, 1985). 1966 to 1972 was probably the last period of activity of fish culture until 1988 when fish farming started again (FAO, 1985). During the military regime of Idi Amin Dada, government departments and fisheries extension agents were unable to contact the farmers due to political instability that prevailed almost everywhere in the country (Balarin, 1976). This brought fish farming to a halt in Uganda. This trend continued even in the early 1980s when Obote came back as a leader for the second time. This halt was broken when adventurous farmers started this agricultural system again in 1988 as already stated earlier.

Species Cultivated:

The major species that were cultivated between 1931-1972 could be divided into two main groups: indigenous and exotic. The indigenous species were very few indeed, mainly because when fish farming first started in Uganda, the fisheries experts had no biological knowledge of fish in lakes. The type of fish they introduced into the lakes added to those which were there already (Balarin, 1985). The breeding that took place was between the indigenous and the exotic species. Of all the fish species in ponds, lakes, and rivers, only five could be considered indigenous, namely: *Protopterus, Bagrus, O. escluentus, O. variabilis* and Mormyrus (Balarin, 1985). The biggest number of fish in ponds, rivers and dams are either exotic or hybridized species. These came from outside Uganda and were stocked in lakes and then in ponds. Such species should be considered exotic to Uganda. They were transferred to Kajansi Experimental Station from Lake Victoria. Of those *clarias* occurs more widely spread but only among adventitious fish farmers in subsistence ponds. The most common fish used in rural ponds are supplied by the Fisheries Department. *Mirror carp* was introduced in the country from Israel in 1957 (Balarin, 1985). Other distributed species included *O. niloticus, O. leucostictus, T. zillii* which was considered inappropriate because of its slow growth and small size (Semokula & Mokoro, 1967). There are other species that are

/	SPECIES	COMMENTS	SYSTEM	LOCATION	INDIGENOUS OR
1.	Mirror Carp	Experimental polyculture, spawned in ponds.	ponds	Kajansi	Exotic
2.	T. Zillii	Not suitable for Uganda.	ponds/dams	Many centers	Exotic
3.	Cyprinus Carpio	Successful (doing well).	ponds	Kajansi	Exotic
4.	Oiniloticus	Highly appreciated.	ponds/dams	Kajansi	Exotic
5.	Protopterus	Grows fast.	ponds/dams	Uganda Co. Estate	Indigenous
6.	Clarias Mossambica	Successful, spawns in running water (rivers).	ponds/dams	Kajansi	Indigenous
7.	O. esculentus	Poor growth, not good for Uganda.	ponds/dams	Kajansi	Indigenous
8.	Ragrus docmac	Successful in ponds.	ponds	Kajansi	Predator cont of tilapia
9.	Micropterus Salmoides	Tilapia predator-control.	ponds	Kajansi	Tilapia preda trials
10.	T. rendalli	Experimental.	ponds	Kajansi	Exotic
11.	Oveochromis variabilis	Very good for Uganda.	ponds/dams	Kajansi	Indigenous
12.	O. Mossambicus	Hybrid trials.	ponds/dams	Kajansi	Exotic
13.	S. Galilaeus	Acceptable growth.	ponds/dams	Many centers	Exotic

used, but are left in ponds in Kajansi Experimental Station. Species such as *O. Mossambicus*, *O. hornrum* were brought to Uganda from Zanzibar; *O. aureus* from Israel; *O. niger* from Kenya, *O. niloticus* from Lake Rudolf in Kenya, and *T. rendelli* from Kenya. *Procambrus spp.* were also tested. Precambrus is being kept at Kajansi Experimental Station and is sold to Kampala Hotels.

Reasons for the Decline:

There were many reasons for the decline, but the major ones were: (i) change of government that took place in 1971: Right from 1962-1971, Uganda was under a civilian president and as such things in the country remained functioning as they were during the colonial era. But when Idi Amin Dada, a military man, overthrew Dr. Milton Obote in a bloodless coup (1971) things began to change. Many Indians and other experts including the Fisheries Officers, most of whom were expatriates, were repatriated. As they left, there were no people with adequate experience in the country to care for this giant venture of fish farming. The vacuum that was created affected fish farming greatly.

(2) Political instability started: Right from 1963, Uganda had an unstable administration. The first leader, Dr. Milton Obote, had his own agenda when he came into leadership. He hated the Baganda (the people of Buganda Kingdom). Buganda had experienced prosperity even before the colonial administration in Uganda. The biggest hospitals in the country, the biggest universities, and the biggest and the best high schools were in Buganda. All other people from outside came in Buganda to look for jobs and employment. When Milton Obote's administration came to power, he voiced resentment for

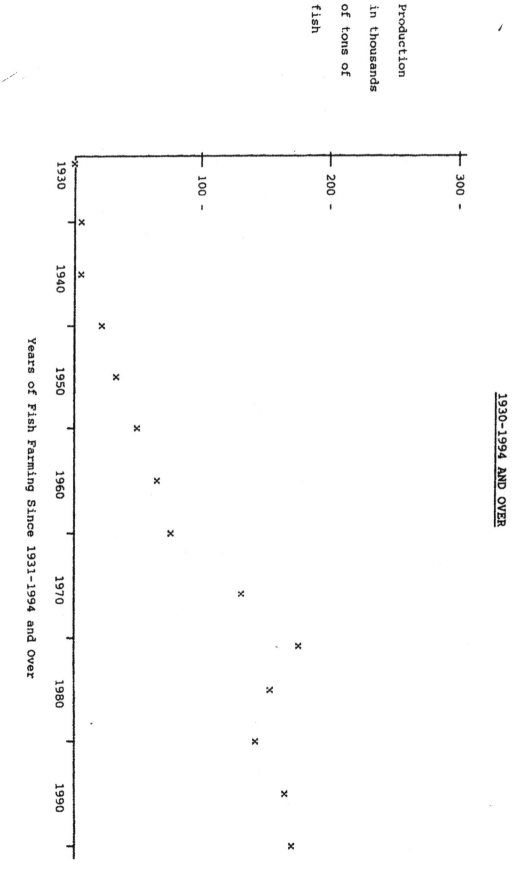

NATIONAL FISH PRODUCTION IN UGANDA

1930-1994 AND OVER

Production

in thousands

of tons of

fish

300 –

200 –

100 –

1930

1940

1950

1960

1970

1980

1990

Years of Fish Farming Since 1931-1994 and Over

the Baganda, although it was they who helped him to come to power. He decided to reduce

the power and the prosperity the Baganda people enjoyed. He decided to deprive them of

their constitutional rights. He reduced the size of Buganda, he passed laws that prohibited the

Baganda from employing people on their farms, and also from having a strong police force,

which enforced law and order in Buganda. He did many other things which were intended to

reduce Buganda's prosperity. This led the Baganda people to resent him too. This hatred

resulted in constant internal conflicts which disrupted peace and stability in the country.

Every sector in the government was affected including Fisheries Department. Thus fish

farming itself started declining and this decline reached its highest peak during Idi Amin

Dada's administration from 1971-1979.

(3) Lack of adequate training of fish guards: Originally, Fisheries Extension Agents

were called fish guards (Kizza, 1993). Many fish guards had formal education. Usually the

people that were recruited to become fish guards had to have a high school certificate of

education. He had to pass science subjects such as physics, chemistry, biology, mathematics,

and other relevant science courses. Fish guards were not in any way trained fisheries

personnel as they only had general education background, and not specific training in fish

farming. These were the people who were sent to work with farmers in rural areas. Because

fish guards were not adequately trained people, they had very little advice to offer the fish

farmers. Thus farmers sometimes started fish ponds without proper technical and education

advice. Many mistakes were made in pond construction, maintenance, the fertilizing of

ponds, in fish feeding, and fish harvesting and cropping.

Because organized fish farming started on a wrong path, it could not survive for long. Because fish took a long time to fully develop, there was less fish production since fish feeding was minimal or almost non-existent. Because ponds lacked proper maintenance, there were many predators. All these affected the overall development of fish farming in the country.

(4) Lack of proper transport: Fish guards were fewer than were needed, and those few who were available were not provided with proper means of transportation. Many could not cover long distances as they were given bicycles to use. As a result, farmers in far away places were ignored. Even the farmers who struggled to maintain their ponds were unable to acquire profit from them, as the farmers did not have appropriate gear to harvest them. Many farmers had maintained their ponds for over twenty years and had not harvested them even once. This discouraged many farmers and led some to eventually give up fish farming (Government Files No. 1/2 Fisheries Department, 1980).

(5) Withdrawal of funds: Fish farming started in Uganda because United Nations, U.S.A., Britain and other nations had donated funds. But when military government came to power, many foreign investors, and other outside countries withdrew funds. This fund withdrawal affected fish farming greatly.

(6) Low wages and salaries: Fisheries Extension Agents were given low wages and salaries. Sometimes this money was not enough to make two ends meet. At times fish guards had to look for additional jobs from which to get supplementary income to meet living requirements. This type of wages and salaries did not encourage fisheries employees to work

hard to promote the development of fish ponds. Due to lack of liveable wages and salaries, fish farming was affected and declined as a result.

(7) Little contact between fish guards and farmers: This was partly due to lack of adequate means of transport and partly due to political instability in the country. This lack of adequate contact influenced the decline in fish farming.

(8) Lack of adequate production of fry: There were few centers to produce fingerlings for distribution to farmers. Most of the experts who worked at fry centers had been deported by Idi Amin's government, so much so that many centers had few well trained nationals to help produce fry for distribution to farmers. This also influenced the immediate breakdown of the fish farming industry in the country.

(9) Poor management: The poor growth rate of stocked fish was due to poor management of fish ponds. There was a lack of supplementary feeding and this reduced the amount of fish in ponds. As fish farming was declining in 1979, Idi Amin Dada was defeated in the Uganda-Tanzania War. He was replaced by Professor Joseph Lule. He was also soon replaced by Godfrey Binayisa. Binayisa was then replaced by Muwanga, who actually assisted Milton Obote to come back the second time in 1980. Obote again was defeated by Okello Lutwa, who was also defeated by Yoweri Kaguta Museveni in 1986. Throughout the whole of this period between 1971-1986, there was almost nothing achieved except fighting and destroying what was there. Most of the infrastructures were destroyed including whatever infrastructural development for fish farming that had been achieved. But after 1986, peace was restored in the country and things began to come back to life again.

Fish Farming District Wise:

Uganda is divided into 39 districts for administrative purposes. Fish farming has

reached in all the 39 districts, but at the time of the investigation, 13 districts had submitted

their statistical figures for 1993. Kitgum has 76 ponds, 36 restocked, but 40 ponds are

unstocked. The species grown in this district are mainly *Oriochromis niloticus* and *Mirror*

carps. According to the report that was sent to the Fisheries Head Office at Entebbe, most

ponds in this district are doing well and only a few were fair and a handful were doing bad.

The Extension officials are working hard to promote fish farming, but a few

constraints come their way such as lack of adequate fry supplies. This has led some major

fish farming ponds to close down. In Fortportal, there are 159 ponds, and 86 fish farmers.

All these ponds are stocked. The type of fish grown in this district is *Tilapia* zillii. The total

acreage of fish farming in this district is 70.966 square meters. Extension workers are putting

in efforts to improve fish farming in this district.

Apac is one of the districts found in the Northern regions. There are 23 fish ponds

and all of them are stocked. The species grown in the area are *Tilapia* zillii and *Tilapia*

niloticus. The pond dimensions in the district is 50.68 m2. In 1993, 800 fry were received in

the districts. The fish generally are doing well, but there is a mortality ratio 20.7%.

Extension workers are putting in maximum amount of effort to promote fish farming in the

area.

Toro district has 55 fish ponds, of which 39 are stocked, 16 unstocked. The type of

fish grown in the area are *Tilapia* zillii and *Mirror carps*. Both of these two species are

expensive to grow, *Tilapia* zillii is basically small fish and *Mirror carps* depend on factory

STATISTICAL FIGURES DISTRICT-WISE 1993

Districts	No. of Ponds	Ponds Stocked	Ponds Unstocked	Type of Fish	Area in m^2	Remarks
Jinja	21	0	21	-	8,186.45 m^2	Have difficulty stocking ponds
Kampala	5	5	1	Tilapia zillii 0. Niloticus	1,335 m^2	Fish doing well
Kabale	5	1	4	Oreocromis, Clarias	1,600 m^2	Rehabilitating ponds
Rukungiri	9	0	9	-	-	Have difficulty stocking ponds
Masaka	-	-	-	-	-	Extension office working hard
Kunmi	12	2	10	o. Niloticus Cyprius carpio Tilapia zillii	4,114 m^2	Have all tanks n desalting dams
Kitgum	76	36	40	Oriocromis Niloticus Mirror Carps	-	57% doing well 32% doing fair 5.2% doing bad
Fortportal	159	159	0	Tilapi zillii	70.955 m^2	85 farmers doing well
Apac	23	-	-	Tilapia Niloticus, Tilapi zillii	5.068 m^2	*800 grand total fry received. *12 reserved for mortality during cropping. *20.7% mortality ratio.
Tororo	55	39	16	O. Niloticuc, Tilapia zillii	-	Fish and farmer doing well
Lira	100	65	35	-	-	Transportation problem, office working hard to identify potent farmers
Busenyi	88	61	27	Tilapia zillii	-	Ponds need maintenance; soil ponds are well maintained. 6 stocked dams, 2 valley tanks.
Capchorwa	44	24	20	Mirror carp	-	Type of feeds: maize bran, Malwa residue. Fertilizers: cow, dung, goat, pig, chicken dropping Farmers doing well

manufactured foods which are very expensive. Extension workers are putting in maximum efforts to promote fish farming in the area (Uganda Government Files, 1993).

In Jinja district there are 21 fish ponds totaling to 8,188.45 square meters. They have two valley tanks and no dams are available in the district. The extension workers have difficulty in getting ponds stocked. If the situation continues at this rate, many ponds will be abandoned.

In Kampala district there were five ponds and four of those are stocked. They have a total acreage of 1335 square meters under fish farming. Two types of species grown are *Tilapia* zillii and *Oreochromis niloticus*. The number of ponds are increasing almost every day. Fish farmers come to Kajansi Experimental Station to collect fry for planting in their ponds. The fish are doing well and farmers follow rules in planting and maintaining their ponds as these farmers are close to the Fisheries Department from where they can contact officials who can help them in advising them of what to do (Uganda Government Files, 1993).

Kabaale district has five ponds, one was stocked and four were not. Kabaale is far away from places where to collect fry for planting and this cuts down the number of farmers because of the lack of availability of fry in the area. Extension workers are doing their best to promote fish farming in the district, but the smallness of staff and lack of adequate transportation has reduced the number of farmers in the area. The type of species grown in this district are *Oreochromis clarias* and *Oreochromis niloticus*. The total area under fish farming is 1600 square meters. Plans are underway to rehabilitate fry centers close to the farmers which might increase the number of fish farmers in the area. There is a tendency among fish farmers to have small ponds. They have been advised to enlarge their ponds and also to add inlets and outlets to their ponds. The Extension workers are working hard to promote fish farming, except that farmers tend to overlook the advice. Contacts between farmers and Extension workers are provided with bicycles and such means cannot cover wide areas.

Rukungiri district is also far removed from fry centers. Farmers have been encouraged to construct ponds, but because fry centers are far from the area, no ponds have been stocked.

Masaka district is one of the biggest and at one time, Masaka had very advanced fish farming, but due to political instability, most of the fish ponds were abandoned. The Fisheries Officers are working hard to promote fish farming in the district. The few officers are working hard to identify suitable places for fish farmers to do better fish farming. In submitting the report, the officer forgot to identify the number of ponds in the district. He did not inform the head office of the number of ponds stocked and those which are unstocked (Uganda Government Files, 1993).

Kuumi district has twelve ponds, two are stocked and ten are unstocked. The total acreage under fish farming is 4,114 square meters. The species grown are *Oreochromis niloticus*, *Cyprinus carpio* and *Tilapia* zillii. There are eleven dams in the district and no valley tanks. The dams are in very bad shape as they were abandoned for a long time. They need to be rehabilitated. As these ponds have been abandoned for a long time, they need desilting. Transportation for the Fisheries Officer is very inadequate as many have bicycles and usually the officers are few in number. This cuts down the amount of travelling the officers can do. Many times farmers around the fisheries office will be visited, but those far away will not have contacts. The fry are in the same way difficult to get from far away centers. The fisheries officers at Kajansi Experimental Station are going to encourage farmers in various locations in districts to grow fry for distribution among other farmers. These, however, will be sold rather than be given free as it has been previously done.

Lira district is in the northern region. According to "annual report" that was submitted to the Head Office just before the end of 1993, the officer in the district indicated that they had 100 ponds in the district, that four were stocked, 35 were not stocked, and 61 still need rehabilitation. The officer did identify the type of fish grown in the area. As everywhere in the country, Lira district has transport problems. The officials are working hard to identify potential farmers in the district.

In Busenyi there are 88 ponds, 61 of which are stocked and 27 were unstocked at the time the report was made. The type of species grown in the area is *Tilapia* clarias. They have six dams and two valley tanks. All six of the dams are stocked. None of the valley tanks are stocked. Many ponds need rehabilitation. Some of these were constructed in the 1950s and 1960s, but due to unavoidable circumstances, they fell into disuse. Some ponds, however, are well maintained, some are still in the bush and need clearing. Other ponds at the same time are fenced and fish are well fed. The farmers are working hard to care for their ponds, so as to produce profit from the projects. The Extension workers are working hard to promote fish farming in the district. Sometimes the officers are too few and transportation, at times, is difficult. This influences fish production.

Kapochorwa district is in the south of Karamoja. There are 44 ponds in this district, 24 are stocked and 20 are unstocked. The specie grown is *mirror carp*. This is an exotic specie from Israel and the type of feed used on this specie is factory manufactured. Apart from the manufactured feeds, farmers also use maize bran, malwa residue for feeding their fish in ponds. Farmers also fertilize their ponds using cow-dung, chicken, goat and pig droppings (Uganda Government Files, 1993).

THE REPUBLIC OF KENYA

While the forerunner of modern-day tilapia keeping in ponds began in Egypt in 2500 B.C., fish culture proper was not introduced to Kenya or the rest of Africa until colonial period (1890-1963). In 1924, the first scientifically oriented approach to farming fish for food was initiated in Kenya in *Tilapia* culture (Maar et al., 1966).

After the Second World War, when a decline of protein food supply occurred, the introduction of fish farming was seen as a cheap and easy way to supply protein foods. It was also seen as a way to satisfy European adventurers who travelled to Kenya for big game hunting. Between 1910 and 1960, large numbers of exotic fish, such as *trout, carp,* and *black bass* were introduced to Kenyan waters; fish farming was also introduced to rural communities via the establishment of demonstration or experimental farms and extension agencies (Anon, 1984).

Status and Scope of Aquaculture:

Presently about 5000 freshwater fish ponds covering an area of about 250 hectares are scattered throughout Kenya. Most of these are owned by individual homesteads, schools, communities, and other various institutions. The majority are built through excavation or construction of simple earthen dams across or along streams and riverlets. The availability of cheap labor enable these fish pond constructions.

Cultured species include the *rainbow* and *brown trout*, various *Penaeus shrimp* species, *Tilapia* species such as *O. niloticus* and others, *black bass, common carp,* and *Artemia salina*, which is cultured as feed for prawn and shrimp (Allela, 1985). Additionally, George (1975) describes 56 species of fish and *shellfish* introduced to Kenya and other African countries. These exotic species were introduced to enrich the local fish; to help control malaria, schistamiasis or weeds in reservoirs or irrigation canals, to fill what were considered to be unoccupied niches; and to overcome the problems of some species and produce hybrid species.

For the most part, *Tilapia* has proven to be the hardiest and most frequently produced species; however, during the 1960s-70s, Kenyan farmers became discouraged by *Tilapia's* tendency toward overpopulation in ponds, which results in stunting growth and thus lowering profits. One of the results of this discouragement was a decline in interest in fish farming, except in situations where considerable government support was provided. In addition, some experts suggest that an absence of technical understanding or skills among fish farmers, and their inability to pursue suitable alternatives, such as the cultivation of *carps, calrias* or other indigenous species, led to widespread abandonment of ponds.

Village-level Fish Culture:

Village level fish culture in Kenya is generally small scale and operated by either individual subsistence farmers, artisanal or community groups. The production of fish is generally integrated with other farming systems. Whether fish are cultivated as a sole or part-time occupation, it is often dependent on government funding and support services. Generally, production units are small and the yields are low.

Throughout Kenya, fish are usually cultivated within their natural environment, whereby the natural selection, rather than the human intervention, determines the genetic make-up of most species. While fish are tolerant of a certain range of environmental conditions, the practice of fish culture proper or the establishment of fish culture systems represents an intentional attempt to create a healthy production environment (Balarin, 1984).

As stated earlier, verbal reports indicate that many Kenyan fish ponds have been, in some cases, abandoned and that fish culture is now being practiced on the open lakes, rivers, and a few fish ponds scattered across the land of Kenya. This is possible that reports of this kind need to be checked out.

It is true that little data is available about ponds that have been maintained, and the methods used to do so. Because pond aquaculture have been assumed to represent a reasonable means for Kenyans to build a protein supply or profit-making enterprise, it is very important to investigate the dynamics that contribute to farmer decisions to maintain or abandon ponds.

The Basics of Pond Fish Culture:

In 1960, Kenya was one of the 20 African countries which had established ponds. In addition, there were many fish farmers that practiced fish culture on open lakes, such as Victoria, Turkana, the Indian Ocean and on Rivers Tana and Athi. Some farmers excavated the ponds themselves with the help of family members. Some rich farmers hired young people in the community to dig the ponds.

Typically, the fish are fed three times daily, which, of course, some scientists will consider as overfeeding. But many farmers, because they use green leaves like sweet potato leaves, cassava leaves, yams, beer residues, food wastes, and many other domestic wastes, which can be found everywhere in Kenya, farmers don't find it a problem to get them. Thus they are able to feed their fish three times a day. The feedings occur at morning, mid-day and evenings at sunset. Ponds are fertilized by a variety of methods including organic and inorganic fertilizers which carry with them a range of economic and labor costs.

At present, the total annual fish production is about 80,000 MT. This amount is likely to double as a result of full utilization of all the aquatic resources, including the recently acquired two hundred mile exclusive economic zone within the Kenya coastal waters, the need to grow fish food is constantly increasing due to the increasing population.

Marketing Fish:

While it appears that much of the fish cultivated and sold in Kenya are taken from lakes and rivers rather than ponds, the way fish is marketed by the catchers, traders and salespeople appears to be similar.

Fishermen typically harvest fish at night or in early morning. The traders and salespeople interested in marketing fish travel via cars, vans, or hired taxis to buy fish from the fishermen. They then drive rapidly to the markets in the main cities and other secondary towns. Fish that have been caught from Lake Victoria will be sold in Kisumu, Homa Bay,

Kisii, and Migori. Those from the Indian coast and rivers such as Athi and Tana will be marketed in Mombasa, Voi and other surrounding towns. Some traders will be even more adventurous and transport fish from the coast to Nairobi, or from Lake Victoria to Nairobi.

The success or failure of this trade is primarily dependent on how fast the trader and salespeople are able to sell their fish before they spoil. Not surprising, lack of refrigerated transportation system is cited as a handicap in fish farming.

Experts and Extension Efforts in Aquaculture:

In the early 1960s and 1970s, fish farming in Kenya was at its initial stages and subsistence farmers were the primary producers. Because fish farming was at its initial stages there wasn't serious government scientific research and information transfer that took place. However, a few qualified experts were available to answer questions. These aquacultural experts and scientists worked primarily in universities as professors or worked with the Ministry of Fisheries and Animal Husbandry. These scientists trained Assistant Agricultural Officers, who acted as Extension Agents and worked with farmers on technical problems and production questions. At times, the Assistant Agricultural Officers would contact the scientists to help solve the more difficult problems related to diagnosing diseases, measuring water qualities, using certain types of food, and determining pond shape, size and volume among others.

The Assistant Agricultural Officers were sent everywhere in the country to introduce fish culture information to farmers during the 1960's and 1970's. Farmers occasionally met at the sub-district office headquarter where they were addressed by the officers. Later officers visited farmers individually and discussed with them the sites, size and shape of the planned ponds, among other issues.

After a farmer finished digging a pond, she or he went to the agricultural office to collect fingerlings to plant in the pond. From time to time, the officers visited farmers to see how the fish progressed. Occasionally the officers also planned demonstrations at the agricultural office to demonstrate to the farmers how to feed pond fish and maintain ponds. Farmers were also sometimes instructed in various methods of harvesting fish by nets, seine, and baskets. After the demonstrations, the farmers were encouraged to try these methods themselves. But very few fish farmers were able to buy their own nets because they were expensive. A few dared to try to use baskets or hooks. This type of harvesting resulted into very few fish being caught. Most of the time, farmers waited until Extension Agents brought fish nets from the office and then harvesting, or sampling as it was called, was done.

What is obvious from the above description is the top-down thrust of Kenyan fish farming education efforts from the experts to the Extension Agents, and then to the village-level producers. This top-down information flow is very common in most of the Third World nations projects. But often the yields of such type of information flow is discouraging. Adoption of recommended practices is often influenced by many contextual and economic factors not immediately apparent to the proponents who see the benefits of the practice but are not familiar with the cultural set up in which the projects are to be established. Therefore, gaps in understanding and perspectives often exist between proponents and practitioners. These gaps can be revealed by the type of production that comes from the project or projects.

TANZANIA

Scientific fish farming proper started in Tanzania about 32 years ago. This was about the same time when Tanzania achieved its national independence in 1964. The first important attempt to promote fish farming was completed in 1963. The emphasis was put on efficient exploitation of fish in lakes, rivers, and in inland water bodies like in ponds, dams, reservoirs. These plans had been effected and the fisheries department reported that there was resounding success (UN, 1964).

As aquaculture in Tanzania has been underdeveloped, as it is elsewhere on the African continent, Tanzania Government in its second five years plan (1972-74), emphasis was placed on aquaculture.

There is great opportunity which many African governments have overlooked and it is the development of aquaculture. If this sector of agriculture was well developed, fish would be placed on every individual's table for food. This would reduce greatly the amount of the malnutrited babies and adult people on the continent.

Tanzania has rich potential for aquaculture development. There are innumerable fish ponds, swamps, and large numbers of dams and lakes which could be developed as fisheries resources on the continent. In addition to those water bodies, the brackish water lagoons are highly suitable for shrimp and fish culture. The ocean coastal waters offer good locations for growing fish, such as oysters culture.

Some fish ponds have been made and as per 1968, there were about 8,000 ponds (FAO/UN, 1968). Most of these ponds were small, 4 m x 4.5 m in size. These were mainly used for *Tilapia* species. The efforts made for fish ponds in Tanzania were scanty, scattered and very sporadic. One can find one or two farmers in a village owning fish ponds. At times these farmers are scattered far apart about 15 to 20 miles from each other. Some fisheries and experimental stations have been established such as Korongwe fish farm in Tanga Region. It was constructed in 1950. In more recent years fish culture activities have been initiated at Nyagezi, a freshwater fisheries center. At this station studies in respect to *Tilapia* culture, in ponds, and cages and hybridization have been carried out.

A Japanese survey mission prepared a report regarding the potential and plans for shrimp culture in Tanzania (Marr, 1966). The author has surveyed many places in Tanzania relating to fish farming development in the man made lakes, ponds, dams, reservoirs and irrigation canal. A big project plan in Tanzania about aquaculture development has been done in respect to oyster culture in the coastal waters.

The basic necessity for aquaculture development in Tanzania is the establishment of fish farms on sound basis. The knowledge the experts have in Tanzania regarding fish farming techniques in different water bodies, like ponds, swamps, dams, canals and lagoons is the first and primary necessity. In addition, the availability of adequate fish fry for stocking the water bodies is equally necessary.

The most numbers of fish ponds in the country are small and each farmer constructed his or her ponds according to her or his understanding, but not according to the advice of the fisheries officers. Thus the experts need to discuss the issues related to fish farming with the farmers themselves. Farmers need to know the proper size, type of ponds, and the suitable species that should be cultivated for fish farming project to succeed. Aquaculture can be a dependable occupation if it is properly managed. The fish farming project requires adequate financial support.

Prospects of Aquaculture in Tanzania:

- Vast potential for aquaculture exists in Tanzania which need efficient development of the available resources. This will make it possible to supply protein requirements to the millions of malnutrited children and adults in the country.

- Under the present Tanzanian political system whereby many people live in rural regions far away from locations where fish can be produced easily, fish ponds, dams, reservoirs and artificial irrigation canals would go a long way to enable those rural individuals to acquire fish.

- There are several lakes that are being created as a result of constructing new hydro-electric power projects, some of which would form very excellent fishery environments. These projects would only need stocking of adequate amount of fry which will reproduce to not only provide fish for the population, but would also greatly promote the fisheries trade outside Tanzania.

- It could be added here that most of the failures in fish culture in the country so far can be attributed to lack of knowledge of fish farming. A fish farm at Kingolwira prison farm, around Morogoro township, was reported to be yielding small sized *Tilapia sp.* and the production of fish was discouraging. The ponds were overpopulated. By reducing the population of fish in each pond, the encouraging fish growth was achieved.

- The experimental work on the fish farm, if practiced in Tanzania, would go a long way to rebuild the stocks of certain depleted species such as *Labeo victorianum* in Lake Victoria. This will help to improve the propagation of various highly cultivable species which are not cultivated presently.

Present Status of Fish Farming in Tanzania:

1. Five well-designed fish farms were proposed in 1975-1980. The construction of the ponds on two sites started in 1975 and the third farm was started in 1976. The remaining two farms were started in 1977.

These farms were established for experimental purposes. These farms would help fisheries officers in maintaining, constructing, selecting a site and in stocking, sampling and harvesting of future ponds.

These farms have sets of breeding, rearing, and marketing ponds of different sizes and most of the farms have encouraged future constructions and maintenance of fish ponds in the country.

2. Farms in Morogoro Region. This region has a big number of fish ponds. There are farms such as "Kidatu Reservoirs" constructed in relationship to *Great Ruaha* power project on the Ruaha River. This manmade dam requires adequate stocking to make fisheries viable and therefore the establishment of a manmade fish pond on this site very significant. It has been stocked and a good number of fish are being harvested annually. The site at Kidodi had been considered before Kidatu was established. But because there were many alternative sites the first site was dropped and the second was adopted. There are other sites such as

Kilosa, Ifakara, and Morogoro. Because of insufficient information regarding these sites it is possible that some of these sites might have fallen in disuse. But many of these sites are being used due to the fact that they were stocked around 1977 (Singh, S. B., 1979).

3. <u>Mwanza Region</u>. At Nyageri around Mwanza region, fish farm was established. The fisheries institute at Mwanza was responsible for training the Fisheries officers at Nyagezi. This farm supports the fish culture in the northwest region of West Tanzania. The construction was started in 1975 and was completed after the end of 1976.

4. <u>Nyumba ya Mungu Dam</u>. This was another hydroelectric power station that was to be constructed on River Pangani. The project was completed and a big dam was formed. The stocking of the dam was inadequate, than the harvesting that was carried out. It was necessary to locate a fish farm close by that would be used for fish fry for restocking this dam. The construction of this farm was expected to be completed in 1976 or 1977. The changes in government administration and also the political inclination, from communism to capitalism could have interfered with all these plans. This Mtera reservoir, as it was called, was to be within the Iringa Region. This location has many swamps, fish ponds, and dams which were suitable for fish promotion in the country.

5. <u>Brackish water aquaculture</u>. It was suggested by the Japanese who surveyed the country to establish three fishery farm sites: one at Tanga, another one near Dar-es-Sabaam, and the last one at Rufigi Delta.

(a) The Udofu Creek at Tanga was expected to be completed between 1975-80. The whole project would cover more than 1000 hectares.

(b) Mzinga Creek was to be initiated between 1975 and completed in 1976.

(c) At Rufigi Delta the project was to be a giant one which would cover an area of

about 500-1000 hectare farm. The money had not been worked out for the

project. All these three giant projects were to be completed by 1980.

A comprehensive and a systematic survey of aquaculture in Tanzania has not yet been done.

In 1963 FAO recommended the Southern region of the country to be suitable for

aquaculture (FAO, 1964). Dibbs, in his economic survey, recommended Songea or the

Southern portion of the country to be suitable for fish farming. But in the end, he

contradicted himself when he again stated that fish culture would be good but not the

cheapest. He stated that there were many natural sources of fish like rivers, lakes and other

natural reservoirs. Despite all his recommendations, it was reported in 1968, that there were

8000 fish ponds in Tanzania.

According to Ibrahim (1970) and Ibrahim and Lenea (1972), fish farming in Tanzania

is not uniform throughout the country. Ruvuma and West Lake had more fish ponds

constructed, but many other parts of the country had almost none. They made the following

observations:

(a) That fish farming in Tanzania was part-time job.

(b) Ponds were constructed without technical advice.

(c) Fish farmers lacked techniques of pond management like feeding, fertilizing,

sampling and harvesting.

(d) Systematic pond management is not practiced.

(e) Proper species selection is not done and many species enter fish ponds

accidentally.

(f) Most of the ponds are too small and too shallow.

(g) Most of the ponds have stunted species of *Tilapia* which are supplied to interested fish farmers as fingerlings.

(h) Ponds have not been drained, treated or manured for number of years.

(i) No proper record of fish production was kept. This makes it impossible to assess pond production.

(j) Prisons have good well maintained ponds like at Korogwe in Tanga, have a 30 acres fish ponds, and at Moshi have a 15 acre ponds. They probably have cheap labor. This makes it easy to maintain these ponds well.

(6) <u>Freshwater aquaculture</u>. To this day in Tanzania, there are no proper records regarding fish farming. Even though fish farming has been practiced by private individuals and public institutions like schools and prisons, most of these do not have any production figures. The figures they have only indicates the number of fish rather than the total weight of fish harvested.

Aquaculture has lagged behind in the absence of established fish farms and suitable personnel. As early as 1950, experimental farm was established at Korogwe, Tanga Region. In Tanzania, the following species are being cultivated.

(a) *Tilapia niloticus* taken from Pangani river.

(b) *Tilapia esculenta* taken from Lake Victoria.

(c) *Tilapia variabilis* taken from Lake Victoria.

(d) *Tilapia massambica* introduced from Kenya.

(e) *Tilapia rendalli* (melanopleura) introduced from Zaire.

(f) *Tilapia machrochir* introduced from Zaire.

When *Tilapia nilotica* was introduced in Tanzania and stocked in ponds at 3,000 per acre (7,5000 per hectare). This resulted to 2,400 lb. per year could be received from these fish ponds.

At Moshi where a pond of 0.18 hectares was stocked with 800 fingerlings, in August 1973, 228-450 mgm of fish were harvested from the pond.

Experimental work carried out at the Freshwater Fisheries Institute at Nyagezi indicated that when *T. esculenta* and *T. zillii* fry of 12-15 mm were stocked in a pond of 0.2 acre at a density of 3,600 per acre, the production of 1,772 kg per acre or 4,432 kg were obtained in four months time, and the growth rate of species was excellent.

(7) Fish culture in paddy fish culture. On the fish farm at Korogwe in 1950, some experimental fish culture in paddy fields were carried out in about 7 acres. These experiments produced one ton of paddy rice and 100 lb. of fish per acre per year. The experiments were discontinued (Gould, 1951).

(8) Fish culture in floating cages. One of the most recent discoveries of fisheries was to rear fish in floating cages. The work carried out at Nyagezi has indicated that floating cages of 3.5 x 3.5 x 3.5 m and 5 x 5 x 5 m were fabricated with locally available materials like bamboos, fry, poles, empty drums, and fish nets material could be used to rear *T. esculenta* and *T. zillii*. With supplementary feeding, using beer-dreg, corn meal, green vegetables and domestic food left overs, *T. esculenta* could be developed to marketable size.

(9) <u>Duck-cum-fish culture</u>. The prison authorities in Morogoro are practicing this type of fish culture. The pond is stocked with *T. rendalli* and *Clarias massambicus*. More than 1,000 ducks are also reared close to the pond. The manure from the ducks is used to fertilize and also to feed the fish in the pond and the fish production is very encouraging. According to the figures from this prison authority indicate that this type of fish culture is succeeding.

Year	Quantity of Fish Harvested in Tanz. Sh.	Revenue from Sale of Fish in Tanz. Sh.	Revenue for Sale of Ducks	Total Revenue
1973	2,364	2,514	12,980	15,494
1974	2,670	4,170	7,505	11,675

Source - From Morogoro prison authorities.

(10) <u>Sewage-pond fish culture</u>. This type of fish culture is no longer practiced in Tanzania. This practice is resulting in good fish yield. Large sized fish are being harvested by individuals.

According to Pillay (1993), this type of fish culture should be discouraged. The fish that has been reared in sewage pond tend to harbor viral and bacterial pathogens. This contaminates the fish. When people eat some of this fish food they can easily get diseases in their bodies. Tanzania authorities also decided to stop this type of fish farming. Some people, however, still harvest fish from Kibaha ponds near Dar-es-Salaam. The fish in this pond are not directly in contact with the polluted pond water. But still since the water from sewage pond is itself contaminated, there are chances that fish from these environments are equally contaminated.

Fish Hybridization:

Production of monosex species of *Tilapia* and their use in fish culture has been accepted as one of the methods to overcome overproduction by *Tilapia species*, which result into stunted growth in fish.

Monosex fish culture at Nyagezi has resulted into 100% male hybrids (Ibrahim & Lema, 1974). When male fish only are used in a pond, there will not be any reproduction taking place. The pond itself will be used as a growing area. What you plant in the pond is what you get from there and sometimes less as some of them die.

Species Cultivated in Tanzania:

The fish most cultivated in Tanzania are *Tilapia species, Clarias mossambicus, Bagrus docmac, Lubeo victorianus, Lates niloticus, Burbus spp. Citharinus sp.* and *trout*. According to law in Tanzania no exotic species are allowed into the country. Thus, even the fastest growing species such as *carp*, Indian and Chinese carp cannot be introduced in the country. The introduction of such species in the neighboring countries like Zambia, Malawi, Uganda and Kenya are being watched carefully. One major factor that has led to the poor production of pond fish is the lack of management techniques that are everywhere in all parts of Africa. Fisheries officers should increase their visits to the farmers (Bardach et al., 1972). Another big problem in fish farming is the fingerlings that are stocked in ponds. They are usually taken from those types of fish that have remained in ponds for a long time. Many of them, as a result of overproduction, are stunted. When such species are introduced in ponds, they immediately begin to reproduce profusely. This is not the ideal type of fingerlings in respect to quality.

Methods of breeding of fingerlings of known age and parentage need to be known.

These will result in better fish culture.

List of Species Grown in Tanzania:

Species	Family	Place
1. *Tilapia esculenta*	*T. Cichlidae*	Freshwater
2. *Tilapia nilotica*	*T. Cichlidae*	Freshwater
3. *T. rendalli*	*T. Cichlidae*	Freshwater
4. *T. microchir*	*T. cichlidae*	Freshwater
5. *T. variabilis*	*Cichlidae*	Freshwater
6. *T. mossambica*	*Cichlidae*	Freshwater
7. *T. pangani*	*Cichlidae*	Freshwater
8. *T. jipe*	*Cichlidae*	Freshwater
9. *T. andersonii*	*Cichlidae*	Freshwater
10. *T. ruvumae*	*Cichlidae*	Freshwater
11. *Protopterus aethiopicus*	*Lepidosirenidae*	Freshwater
12. *Clarias massambicus*	*Claridae*	Freshwater
13. *Bagrus docmac*	*Bagridae*	Freshwater
14. *Bagrus spp.*	*Bagridae*	Freshwater
15. *Auchenoganis occidentalis*	*Bagridae*	Freshwater
16. *Schillee mystus*	*Schilloidae*	Freshwater
17. *Labeo victorianus*	*Cyprinidae*	Freshwater
18. *Labeo cylindricus*	*Cyprinidae*	Freshwater
19. *Barbus altianalis*	*Cyprinidae*	Freshwater
20. *Barilius microcephalus*	*Cyprinidae*	Freshwater
21. *Anguilla nebulosa labiata*	*Aquillidae*	Freshwater
22. *Citharinus spp.*	*Citharinidae*	Freshwater
23. *Alestes spp.*	*Characidae*	Freshwater
24. *Hydrocynus spp.*	*Characidae*	Freshwater
25. *Gnathonemus spp.*	*Morminidae*	Freshwater
26. *Mormyrus*	*Morminidae*	Freshwater
27. *Marcusenius spp.*	*Morminidae*	Freshwater
28. Rainbow Trout *salmo-gair dneri*	*Salmonides*	Freshwater
29. Brown Trout *Salmo trulta*	*Salmonides*	Freshwater
30. Black Bass *Salmonides nicropterus*	*Centrarchidae*	Freshwater

MALAWI

Fish farming is relatively low in Malawi. It is basically subsistence in nature. There are a few larger ponds and a few fry production centers established by the government. Malawi is a small landlocked country in Central Africa. Fish is the main source of animal protein in the country.

Fish farming is about 700 ponds scattered across the country. In the north it covers about 100 hectares. The Ministry of Agriculture in Malawi offers assistance and advice regarding the stocking of *Tilapia shirana* in ponds. Over 50 hectares in the country are stocked with *cichlids* and sometimes with *Black bass, micropterus salmonides* for food production and a little sport fishing.

Sport fishing is strongly encouraged by the government in highland forest and game reserves with *Rainbow trout*. Large scale fish farming is at experimental level on an irrigation farm in the southern lowlands over 20 hectares. *Tilapia* and other species are grown on this farm.

Malawi produces about 50 MT of fish annually. The government is doing everything in its power to recover the small shallow Chilwa lake which dried up. Over a million fish fry were stocked, but when sampling was conducted, it was revealed that this had very little effect on the recovery of the lake. About 700-1000 subsistence fish farmers are involved as part-time workers. Fish farming in Malawi is integrated with other agricultural systems such as crop farming, animal husbandry, poultry farming, etc. There are no farmers in Malawi who deal with fish farming by itself.

Estate dam management occupies 30 to 40 workers and fish farming in drainable ponds employs 15 more workers. Sport fishing hatchery and control occupies ten men and the prawn culture will employ another ten workers. In all 110 workers are employed on this experimental farm.

Species Cultivated:

Name	Remarks
Tilapia shirana boulanger *T.S. Chilwae* and *T.S. Shirana* *T. Melanopleura A. Dum*	Commonest in culture in country.
T. rendallii Boulanger *T. mossambicus* (Burchell)	Often in mixed culture.
Clarias Mossambicus (Burchell) *Serranochromis robustus* (Gunther)	Often adventitious carnivores in mixed cultures.
Micropterus Salmonides - Black Bass	In reservoirs introduced in country from Rhodesia.
Salmo gaird-nerrii (Richardson) - Rainbow Trout	From South Africa.
Protopterus annectens (Owen) *Lung fish*	Adventitious and profitable.
Macrobranchium resenbergii (de Mann) Dawe prawn	Introduced in 1973 from Thailand. No effect yet.

Aquaculture Centers:

Type of Center	Type of Culture	Location
Large ponds 1-4 ha, drainable	*Tilapia spp.* (monosex), polyculture, *Tilapia spp., serranochromis sp., protopterus sp.*	Kasinthula
Estates of small ponds, drainable	As above, excluding monosex and *protopterus sp.*	Mulanje, Zomba, Bunda, Mzuzu
Reservoirs, managed, with drainable 1-20 ha	*T. melanopleura, T. Shirana, micropterus salmoides*	Throughout the country, mainly in south
Subsistence ponds, not drainable, 1/10 - 1/2 ha. Experimental prawn ponds, trout hatchery	*T. shirana, serranochromis sp., Macrobranchium sp., Salmo gairdnerii*	Throughout the country, mostly north. Zomba (Domasi), Zomba, Viphya, Nyika plateaux.

Fish Farming Practices:

Monosex culture is practiced. *T. melanopleura* and *T. shirana* are stocked at 6,000 ha. Ponds are fertilized using superphosphates. Fish are fed with maize bran, yam meal, cooked and raw at 5% of body weight daily. No disease control is practiced apart from the regular examination. Management and maintenance is done by FAO officials, the supervisor and his assistant. These are assisted by a labor force of five men.

Mixed cultures of *T. shirana, T. melanopleura* and *serranochromis sp.* and *Clarias sp.* are conducted at 90-95% herbivores, and the rate of stocking are 10,000/hectares. The yield from these ponds is now exceeding 2,000 kg/ha as feeding and stocking methods have improved greatly. Sampling of ponds is conducted over five months. A one month fallow is skipped between each harvest. According to *T. shirana's* growth rate and harvesting, it has been identified that three to four fish farming crops can be carried out.

<u>Dams and Reservoirs</u>:

Stocking varies from reservoir to reservoir and from dam to dam. Many of these water bodies, as it were, are neglected. Fertilizing and feeding among local farmers is many times ignored. Disease control as such is almost not thought of. These ponds, dams, reservoirs are not drainable and are only harvested using angling or using hooks. There are a few farmers, however, who can manage to afford fishing nets. In such cases, these do harvest their ponds regularly. But there are some who have nets, but do not know how to use them and as such ponds are not harvested. Because of this poor maintenance of these ponds, there is a substantial financial loss on the side of the farmers.

It is vital that fisheries officers or Extension Agents educate farmers along the lines of maintaining their fish ponds which will not only increase their fish production, but will save them a lot of frustrations.

Fish ponds in Malawi range from 0.1 to 0.5 hectares. The government does the stocking of the already made ponds. The fisheries officers know the scientific methods of transferring fingerlings from the place of production to the locations of stocking. These fingerlings are sometimes not examined carefully. Some of these fingerlings turn out to be predators which become detrimental to the farmers by consuming the fish in ponds.

Some farmers occasionally through negligence or ignorance feed their fish in ponds and use kitchen wastes, banana leaves, cassava or potatoes. This kind of feeding is often impossible to evaluate because the information is not readily available. As stated, area disease control is non-existent. Control of disease among fish farmers is little or non-existing. Harvesting is usually by nets or angling using hooks weekly. Yields from these ponds is usually 150-200 kg per hectare. Costs of such operations are maintained when labor factors

are ignored. Pond labor merges with other farm duties. These duties and responsibilities are

carried out by one member of the farmer's family.

Fish farming in Malawi is unprofitable not because it cannot make a profit, but

because it is carelessly carried out.

ZAMBIA

Fish farming in Zambia started in the 1940's and at present there are over 3000 fish

ponds of about .25 ha each. Zambia produces 3-4 MT per year per hectare. Zambia is a

landlocked country with vast water resources covering an area of 53,680 km. Currently the

population in the country consumes over 80,000 MT, but the total production in the country is

about 62,000 MT (Huisman, 1985). Fish culture, mainly in ponds, has contributed to over

700 MT per year. The amount imported in from the surrounding countries is small. In 1958,

the government constructed six ponds in Chilanga which became demonstration units. At the

end of 1965, there were 1231 ponds with an approximate area of 100 ha. Most of these

ponds were owned by subsistence farmers who grew fish for their domestic consumption.

At present the government has 19 demonstration fish farms across the country. The

research centers are located at Chilanga, Mwekera and Chipata.

The government, assisted by the United Nations Development Programs, the Food and

Agriculture Organization, is emphasizing the improvement of management so as to increase

production per hectare yield. These efforts are helping to improve the commercial and the

village level production. The most current information indicates that there are over 3169 fish ponds and 545 dams in Zambia, but it has been proved through research that with good

management fish farming can be increased.

Species Cultivated:

Fish species grown in Zambia include *T. rendalli*, or *T. melanopleura*; *Oreochromis*

macrochir, O. mossambicus, O. andersonnii, Cyprinus carpio, Serranochromis robustus,

Haplochromis mellandi and *Clarias spp*. Some of these species were introduced in Zambia

for sport fishing and others were stocked in ponds as predators to control the prolific

reproductive potential of *Tilapia sp.* *H. mellandi* was also introduced to control snails in case

of bilharzia outbreaks in ponds and dams. The *Common carp* was brought in from Malawi in

1980 (Huisman, 1985).

The Government and FAO have been trying and are still trying to identify indigenous

species that could be grown locally. *Oreochromis andersonnii* with its good growth rate and

it does not reproduce as fast as *Tilapia species* do. Various fish farming systems such as fish-

cum-pig culture, fish-cum-duck culture and fish culture using supplementary feeding have

indicated that *O. andersonnii* can be utilized for commercial purposes. Researches that have

been conducted showed that 9.8 MT per hectare per year with pigs, 7.0 with ducks, and 3.6

with intensive feeding. Fish fry that were stocked weighed 20 and 25 grams and fish weighed

100-150 gram at harvest time.

Mirror carp is grown in government farms and has shown impressive results of about

143 grams per months using intensive feeding. Although no definite feed has been

formulated but feeds such as maize bran, rice bran, vegetables, chicken litter, sunflower cake, brewery wastes, slaughter house waste, soybean cake and even poultry feeds are being used at 5% of fish body weight daily.

Due to the factor that natural fisheries cannot satisfy the demand for fish that exist in Zambia, the government has started fish farming to probably help supplement the natural fisheries supply. The government has established fish fingerlings supply program and it is hoped that the government might turn its demonstration centers into fish fry production centers in near future.

The seed production might save the fish industry into development. The difference that is being met by imports could be produced through intensive and integrated fish farming by private and public sectors working together. At present, the international agencies, such as FAO, UNDP, UNHCR and ICMC are working side by side with the Zambian government in furthering the development of the fish farming industry.

In Zambia, fish farming is emphasized to supplement production from the natural waters. Intensive methods of fish farming are now being tried.

The government of Zambia operates experimental fish farms at Chilanga, Mwekera and in other fourteen fish cultures throughout the country.

Chilanga Fish Farm

There are two types of ponds at Chilanga.

(i) Three excavated ponds and no concrete used. These are usually termed natural ponds. These ponds are about .5 hectares and some a little smaller than this. They are about 150 cm deep. Each pond is provided with a sluice, it can be emptied or filled at anytime.

(ii) Concrete pools. These are four ponds built side by side. The ponds are approximately 10 m by 20 m with depth of about 150 cm. These have no sluice and so can only be emptied by pumps. Once the pond is filled, a lot of bundles of grass are thrown on the pond to generate proper biological conditions. The application of the grass improves the oxygen and pH content. This establishes the amount of plankton in the pond. The oxygen content varies from day to day according to the amount of heat temperature for that particular day. The normal oxygen content after the application of fertilizer is about 8.5 ppm.

In the large natural ponds at Chilanga in the dry seasons, the water dries up completely sometimes, but when it rains the water level will be maintained. The water level in these ponds is dependent on whether there is rainfall or not. Thus, the production periods in some of these ponds is limited to some seasons when the country experiences rainfall. During these dry seasons, the bottom of these natural ponds are cleaned. They are dug and the mud, rubbish and weeds which may not be useful to fish are removed.

Mwekera

There are two types of fish ponds at Mwekera. (i) The ponds that are constructed with impervious clay soil. These are about 0.5 ha each and have depth of 120 cm. (ii) Ponds built in black soils each about 20 m by 30 m with a maximum depth of about 120 cm. Both sets of ponds are supplied with water from a nearby dam. The water supply is good enough to allow a year round production of fish in these ponds. These ponds at Mwekera allow water to run through continually and as such, fertilizer cannot be used very often. Because these ponds cannot be allowed to dry out, the pond bottoms cannot be cleaned.

Fertilizers are obtained from Lusaka depot of the National Agricultural Marketing Board. This is a corporation established by the government of Zambia to help the agricultural industry to supply:

(i)   Sodium nitrate (16%) N as Na Noz;

(ii) Triple super phosphate (44% Pas P_2O_5);

(iii) Potassium chloride (60% K as Ku).

(iv) Agricultural lime was used only as disinfectant. Fertilizers were spread by a shovel from the shore, or from the middle of the pond by plunging into the water or, in case of very large ponds, from a boat. They avoided spraying on the rooted and aquatic vegetation to try and avoid too much plant growth in the pond. The fertilizer was spread using a boat daily until the water became of a green color indicating that the water was ready to produce plankton.

Fish in those ponds at Chilanga and Mwekera had a mixture of four species of *Tilapia andersonii, T. macrochir, T. Mortimeri* and *T. rendelli*. In order to achieve high yields, high stocking rates of 5000 pieces to 16,000 pieces of fish were stocked per hectare. The weight of the individual stock fish ranged from 10 to 28 grams. But at the harvest time the fish weighed 142 to 285 grams.

The fish at Chilanga were fed on plankton. They were divided into the following species:

Phytoplankton -   (i)   *Anapaenopsis tanganyika*
                   (ii)   *Cosmarium bolytis manegh*
                   (iii) *Microcystic aeruginasa Kuetz*

Zooplankton -   (i)   *Brachinus sp.* votifera
                   (ii)   *Macrochrix sp.* cladocera
                   (iii) *Cyelops fimbriatus* copepuda

Fish production at Mwekera averaged 185 kg per hectare annually. When fertilization was used, production increased to 820 kg per hectare annually. The constant flow of water through the ponds, the poor soil in some ponds and the accumulation of too much silt on the bottom without periodic cleaning inhibited high production. Because the production at Chilanga were more favorable than those at Mwekera, it was indicative that fish ponds would be better as breeding places if they had concrete surface at the bottom and sides. This would hinder silt from accumulating and turbidity would be avoided. The fertilizers could easily be controlled and so the fish production could be easily evaluated.

It is significant to know that at Mwekera and Chilanga farms and probably in other fish farms in Africa, fish should be fed and ponds be fertilized.

(1) Because organic matters are important for production of fish in ponds, the ponds must be drained periodically and should be allowed to dry to restore vitality. The mud or silt at the bottom must be removed. This makes the water clear and clean for fish production.

(2) Fertilizers settle to the pond bottoms rapidly, it should be spread all over the pond and not at the margins or from only one end.

(3) Feed should not be added or spread over the water dry, but rather should be mixed with some water and be placed at specific feeding locations of the pond.

(4) Before stocking the pond, the number and weight of the fish must be known. This will help evaluate the growth rate.

(5) For good production both good fertilizers and good feeds must be used.

Every year Zambia consumes more fish than what its natural waters can produce. At present, Zambia imports over 20,000 tons. This amount of fish could be produced in ponds in Zambia.

NIGERIA

Fish farming has been practiced in Nigeria for a long time. It has not been on a commercial level, but rather on village level fish culture. Production of fish in the flood plains has been going on for centuries, but modern fish culture practices were started fairly recently. The northern Nigerian government started an experimental fish farm at Ponyam near Jos in 1951. The aim for this experimental farm was to grow the *Common carp*. Fish pond construction was also encouraged by the governments of Western and Eastern Regions. The Federal Government of Nigeria requested for the development of brackish water fish cultures. This was initiated in the Niger Delta area in 1965 by FAO and a second project was established in Lagos in 1968.

Numerous ponds have been started across the country. There is great potential for aquaculture in Nigeria, but the village level fish culture is rather negligible. Estimated annual production of fish in the country is less than 10% from fish pond production. There has been generation of fish ponds and fish farms all over the country.

There is great potential of fish culture in Nigeria but its present contribution to the domestic fish production is rather low. The estimated 700,000 MT, only 10% of that comes from fish ponds (FAO, 1968).

Present Status of Fish Culture:

About 2,000 fish ponds exist in Nigeria. These are owned by communities, schools, institutions, co-operative societies as well as individual fish farmers.

Majority of these ponds are constructed by placing earthen dams across the streams and other rivers. 750,000 to about one million hectares in Nigeria are still available for fish farming mainly in delta area. This location could be potential for fish culture in the continent. Now fish culture is practiced in brackish waters. In Nigeria, fish pond farming is a part-time venture. It is estimated that about a half of a million people are involved in fish farming. In some governments, experimental and demonstration fish farms have well trained extension staff who can supervise fish pond construction and management. In many states, however, the staff is inadequate and lack the necessary training for extension work. Today in Nigeria, there are five research officers, 20 fisheries officers, 60 technical assistants and 200 junior workers employed in aquaculture. These figures change constantly.

Species Cultivated:

Species grown in Nigeria are listed below:

	Species	Water Quality	Remarks
(a)	*Tilapia spp., T. Nilotica, T. milanopleura, T. galilea*	Fresh water sp.	These are preferred sp.
(b)	*Cyprinus carpio*	Freshwater sp.	Transported from Israel or European carp.
(c)	Three varieties: *Cyprinus carpio var specularis, Cyprinus carpio var. nudia*	Freshwater	
(d)	*Heterotis sp.*	Freshwater	Very good for Nigeria
(e)	*Labeo sp.*	Freshwater	Uganda, Nigeria
(f)	*Gymnarchus sp.*	Freshwater	Does well in Nigeria
(g)	*Lates niloticus* (Niger perch)	Freshwater	Does well in most African waters.
(h)	*Clarias sp.*	Freshwater	Exotic in Nigeria, but does well.
(i)	*Chrysichthys nigro digitatus* (catfish)	Brackish water	Very unique in Nigeria.
(j)	*Hemichromis fasciatus*	Brackish water	Grows well in Southern and Eastern part of Nigeria.
(k)	*Lutjanus spp.*	Brackish water	Does well in all country.
(l)	*Gymnarchus sp.*	Brackish water	Does well in all country.
(m)	*Elops sp.*	Brackish water	Most part of Nigeria.
(n)	*Ethmalosa fimbriala*	Brackish water	Fairly good in maturing.
(o)	*Penas duorarum*	Brackish water	Does well in Nigeria and many countries in Africa.
(p)	*Macrobrachium sp.*	Brackish water	
(q)	*Mugil spp.* (mullets)	Brackish water	

Mullets or *chrysichtys* plus *Tilapia* has been found to be ideal for polyculture.

Fish Farming Centers

1.   <u>Hatcheries and Breeding Centers</u>: Some of the states in the country have fisheries divisions which raise fish seeds or fingerlings and distribute them to governments and private farms. There are plans to do more of these in the future.

2.   <u>Pond Farms</u>: These are of different sizes which range from one hectare to about 400 hectares. Some of the farms in the Western and Midwestern states are of this magnitude.

3.   <u>Man-Made Lakes and Reservoirs</u>: These are very significant in Nigeria in regard to freshwater fish production. The water reservoirs and lakes are stocked by government fisheries departments and the local residents make use of these water bodies. The local residents have to have licenses to operate on these reservoirs.

4.   <u>Cages</u>: These are purely for research and experimental purposes. These are being used by the Federal Department of Fisheries and the local Kainji Lake Research project.

Sources of Fry:

Fish fry and fingerlings are obtained from:

(a) Natural waters such as estuaries, lagoons and rivers provide species including mullets, snappers (*Lutjanus spp.*), *Hemichromis spp.*, *Clarias spp.*, *Chrysichthys spp.*, and *Tilapia spp.*

(b) <u>Pond</u>: Species such as Carp, Tilapia, Clarias fingerlings are obtained from government demonstration and breeding centers.

(c) Induced breeding by hormone: This is only done in only few government facilities in Nigeria, but plans are that if fish farming has to go commercial, the use of hormone to induce breeding has to be adopted. This will help to enhance the breeding of *Chrysichthys nigrodigitatus* which cannot be induced easily by natural means in ponds, dams and other manmade water bodies. This issue still requires further research. Hatchery operations are practiced in some parts of Nigeria for the common carp, and *Cyprinus carpio*.

(d) Importation of fry: Apart from the carp fry that were imported into the country in the early fifties, Nigeria does not import any fish fry at all. Whatever they prefer can be produced within the country. It is expected that the governments might bring in the grass carp, *Tenophoryngodon idella*, to try and combat weeds problems in ponds.

Aquaculture Practices:

(i) Stocking rates: Combination of various species and their densities to exploit all food strata in ponds is being worked out in different experimental ponds.

(ii) Feeds and fertilizers: Information on the amount of fertilizers and foods needed is very inadequate. Most private ponds are stocked with fry, but no fertilizers or supplementary feeding is given. The government farms receive fertilizers and feeds. Feeds used in Nigeria include groundnuts cake, spoilt ground nuts, palm kernel cake, rice bran, guinea corn/sorghum and maize.

(iii) Harvesting as of now:

(a) The average recorded harvesting for private farms or ponds is about 750 kg/ha mainly from *Clarias* and *Tilapia spp.*;

(b) Production from experimental ponds with or without fertilizers and supplementary feeds are given below.

Harvesting of Fish, With or Without Fertilizers and Feeds

Species	Water Quality	With Fertilizer Only	With Feeds Only	With Fertilizer and Feeds	Neither Fertilizer nor Feed
1. Common Carp	Freshwater	1024 kg/ha	1600 kg/ha	2030 kg/ha	not applicable
2. Catfish *Tilapia* mullets	Brackish water	200 kg/ha	2400 kg/ha	3000 kg/ha	879 kg/ha

Fish production from private commercial ponds, which do not receive as much care will be even lower than the figures in the table above. The national average is shown in the table below. The figures could be a bit higher as those shown in the table are a little bit outdated, for they were for 1974.

Type of Culture	Natural Production	With Fertilizer	With Supplementary Feed and Fertilizer
Monoculture kg/ha	560	1120	2240
Polyculture kg/ha	670	1350	2690

Social and Economic Prospects:

The figures in the above table are based on fish ponds operated by government. The experiments that were carried out on the government farms show clearly, that an acre of water can produce more proteins than an acre of land. In a well managed fish ponds, up to 3000 kg of fish can be obtained from a hectare annually. The production of 3000 kg per hectare per year is more than four times the production of cowpeas and about three times that of groundnut on the same space of land of one hectare.

<u>Comparative Production of Agricultural Commodities and Fish Per Hectare:</u>

Crops	Yield kg/ha	Cost/kg/KDBO	Value of prod./ha
Rice	1,204.8	24.36	293.48
Cassava	13,332.0	8.0	1,066.56
Yam	10,644.0	12.62	1,343.27
Millet	673.2	7.9	53.16
Cow peas	480.0	24.36	116.93
Groundnuts	903.6	6.36	57.46
Fish:			
Mullets/carp	3,000.0	50.0	1,500.00
Others	500.0	40.0	200.00

Source: Agricultural crops: Federal Department of Agriculture Publication 1971-72.

For fish: Federal Department of Fisheries, and Research Station Papers.

<u>Fish Farming Development</u>

The factors such as land, labor and capital do not constitute major fish farming problems. The major problem is lack of technical skills. Educated people and non-educated millions have been ear-marked for aquaculture development and research in the country budget. This amount is about 10% of the total capital granted by the Government to Fisheries Department. The program includes the stocking of a half million hectares of irrigation, as well as constructing modern fish farms in different parts of the country. The government is willing to invest more money in aquaculture providing that profitability could be demonstrated. FAO experts visited Nigeria and have made recommendations if followed could promote aquaculture in the country. The recommended fish farming techniques if adopted, would assist in the planning of large scale fish farming in Nigeria.

SOUTH AFRICA

In South Africa, aquaculture in the 1980s was significant. The production rose from 345 MT to 3000 MT in 1988. This earned South Africa R 45 million. Seventy percent of all aquaculture undertakings were started five years or ten years back.

Mussels now account for half of the total production in the country. Trout takes second place, accompanied by water hawthorn, oyster and catfish. In terms of value ornamental fish are third in bringing in foreign exchange (Wyrand Vys, Britz, Hacht, 1992).

The total production of pond fish farming compared to the total fish farming production is very small. The amount of fish farming within five years or so increased four times. The business owners in South Africa have to struggle with many factors in the surroundings and the energy nature of South African coastline, but the improvement that has been made is great and does suggest that success of fish farming is indeed possible.

In 1984, only three types, rainbow trout, oysters and water hawthorn were cultivated for human consumption on any appreciable scale. Six species of fin fish, one aquatic macrophyte and six species of mollusks are currently farmed on a commercial basis (De Moor, Bruton, 1989).

Perhaps the most significant thing occurred in 1982 when the Foundation for Research and Development of the Council for Scientific and Industrial Research chose an aquaculture working group to study the potential of fish farming in South Africa to determine the research needs of the industry. The organizational structures and the research supports have promoted fish culture industry throughout South Africa (Uys, Britz, Hecht, 1992).

Coastal Fishing in South Africa

South Africa catches more fish than any other country of Africa. All of these fish come from sea and very little from rivers and lakes. As South Africa had high level of technical development in the country, South Africa has various advantages for fishing.

South Africa is surrounded by slow moving coastal waters known as currents. On the eastern side, we have the warm Agulhas current. It is warm because the water flows from the Equator to the poles. On the western side, we have the Cool Banquela currents, as it flows northwards from the cooler polar region. These currents are very significant for the fishing grounds along the coast. These regions have a lot of fish foods known as plankton. These are microscopic living creatures of the sea. These small living creatures act as food for fish. They collect in regions of the sea where the water is clear, shallow, cool and moving.

Of the two currents, the Banquella current attracts plankton more than the East Agulhas current. Both currents have fish, but Banquella current on the western side of the coast of Africa attracts more insects to it than the Agulhas.

Banquella is 140 km wide and flows at about 30 km per day. The growth of plankton in the current is assisted by the offshore winds when these winds blow, the water is moved away from the coast. This allows the water from the bottom to rise. It brings nutrients with it. These nutrients especially phosphates and nitrates. The nutrients encourages the growth of plankton. These planktons can be divided into plants and animals. The offshore winds are also sometimes disadvantageous as they create big ocean waves which make ocean fishing impossible. Some of these winds create fog.

Areas where fish can be caught in large numbers are called fishing grounds (Turner, 1986). Most fishing grounds along the coast of South Africa are near the continents and are not in mid-ocean.

The sea floor where the ocean is less than 200 mm deep is known as the continental shelf. Most of South African fishing grounds are on the continental shelf along these two ocean currents.

Fishing Methods

Fish of the ocean can be divided into two main groups: One group includes all the fish which live on, or near to, the bottom of the sea. These are the "demsersal fish" which can be caught using "trawling". The second group living near the surface and are called pelagic fish. These are usually caught by purse-seine nets (Turner, 1986). The trawling is divided into two groups. One group is one where fish is caught far out into the mid-sea. This uses larger vessels. The nets are inside the trawl and can be pushed into it again. The trawl is a bag-like. It is smaller, elongated at one end and is broader and around the edges are the metal rollers. At the broader and the net is pushed in and pulled out of the trawl. The trawl is made up of wooden floats. The trawl is suspended into the water deep by using long wire ropes. Wooden boards are connected to these nets to keep them at the bottom of the ocean. The wire ropes are attached to the boat on the surface of the ocean. These large offshore vessels can stay at sea for several days or weeks. They have equipment to preserve fish by freezing it. This reduces the temperature to $0°$ C so that fish are frozen solid, and stops bacterial activity.

The second method is by 'purse-seine nets'. These are used to catch pelagic fish or feet close to the surface. The nets are laid from a fishing boat at sea and not from a beach. A smaller boat is towed behind the fishing vessels and is sued to lay the net, so that a shoal of fish is encircled. The net is then hauled to the side of the vessel by closing the circle and closing the bottom. The fish are then sucked out by a machine. If fishing was not controlled, these waters in South Africa would be overfished. But the government of South Africa has a policy to conserve fish. This helps to keep fish to continue to be in large numbers. The holes of the nets are strictly controlled. This helps smaller immature fish are not caught. They pass straight through the large holes of the nets. No fishing is allowed in some areas which are important breeding places for fish. No pelagic fish are allowed to be caught between September and December. Fish vessels must have fishing licenses from the Fisheries Department. All these regulations and many other unmentioned qualities have made South Africa the largest fish producing nation on the African continent.

CHAPTER V

PROBLEMS THAT HINDER AQUACULTURE

DEVELOPMENT IN AFRICA

There are innumerable constraints to aquaculture in Africa, but a few that are known pose great fear to culturists. Some of these constraints deserve to be, but some are man made. Many of these cause fears among fish farmers because aquaculture profitability is impossible as a result of these problems. These constraints are categorized into three main groups: technical, social and educational.

Technical Problems

Aquaculture in specific areas can be an effective strategy leading to improved economic and nutritional status of the local residents. This has happened in India, Singapore, Hong Kong, Taiwan, Korea, Malaysia, Philippines and Indonesia. Aquaculture, however, has failed to effectively improve the nutritional and economic aspects of the African people. There are many individuals in Africa who have participated in fish farming for many years, but have discovered that fish farming is not profitable as they once expected, and therefore have decided to abandon it.

In Third World nations, particularly in Africa, pond construction is difficult. Constructing a pond is energy demanding, which requires a lot of muscular power. The government policies in various nations is to improve methods currently used to dig ponds. Many African countries are trying to introduce tractors to various locations in their respective nations which farmers can use to excavate the ponds. This will help to increase the number of fish ponds on the continent.

At present many countries cannot afford to buy these tractors, because they do not have foreign exchange to effect the importation of foreign machinery. The factor that fish ponds are difficult to construct and that foreign exchange is a problem for many countries, it is no wonder fish pond construction still remains a problem. The fewer the ponds, the less the profits.

Fish ponds everywhere in Africa are poorly maintained. There is lack of proper fish nutrition. Thus poor growth rate results into fish, such as *Telapia zillii* to take too long to mature. Some of these species are always slow to mature, but situations can be worsened when they are poorly fed. The longer they take to mature, the more costly they become in terms of feeds and general maintenance and this results into profitless ventures. When fish farmers persist on taking care of these fish ponds and seeing no profit out of them for many years, they eventually turn to ventures that will bring profits. But in case these tractors come into the country, they will assist farmers to increase the number of ponds. The more ponds a farmer possesses, the more profit he or she is likely to generate.

There is a shortage of fish fry almost everywhere among fish farmers in Africa. Some farmers can afford to dig ponds, but when they go to Fisheries Centers to collect fry, they find none. This does not only discourage farmers from the venture, but it also makes them hate fish farming per se, as it has lots of problems to overcome and yet, there is only minimal or no profit at all.

The governments across the continent are trying to introduce new methods of fish fry productions by selecting farmers from various locations in their respective nations. These will produce fish fry and increase the amount available to farmers. The farmers will be encouraged to dig more ponds and stock them with fish. More fish will be produced and eventually more profit will be received from these ventures. These farmers will be encouraged to produce as many fish fry as possible and sell to farmers. These farmers will be producing fish fry only and will not produce any other type of fish. As their fish fry production will expand, they may also participate in other types of fish just like other culturists. It has been found in Uganda and in many other East African nations that fish fry is a big hindrance to fish production (Kigeya, 1993).

In many places organic industrial wastes contribute to pollutions of waters in ponds, dams, rivers and lakes by causing turbidity and oxygen depletion. In some places farmers are using these industrial wastes to their advantages by processing agricultural products such as cereals like rice-bran, maize-bran, oil cakes, coconut wastes, wastes from dairy industry and slaughter houses can be used for pond fertilization and for fish feeds too. These pollutions affect fish production greatly, mainly when fish take in some minute particles into their gills. Diseases affecting fish gills will result. Oxygen depletion will affect fish in water. Fish will grow normally if oxygen supply is available. But when oxygen supply is cut short because of turbidity in water, the fish will be affected. The fish will be weakened and will not feed or play normally in water. This will even lead to many fish to die if oxygen supply is not provided in time. Industrial waste can also cause pathogenic bacterial diseases which will be spread to fish in these contaminated water bodies. When such bacterial diseases are spread to fish, they will also spread to human beings who consume these sick fish. As more and more fish become sick, the culturist may destroy the whole stock and try to clean the pond using lime and then restock. In many parts of Africa fish farmers have not reached the sophistication of destroying the whole stock and then restocking. What many people do will be to sell all the fish in the pond and give up the pond. This is another technique of treating the pond. If such a pond is left to rest for some time, the source of industrial waste which originally destroyed the pond may be changed. After some years, the farmer will clear the pond and restock it. Other inexperienced farmers will just give up the pond completely for fear that if he tries again fish will be attacked. In many places in Africa, many ponds, dams, lakes, rivers, reservoirs and irrigation canals are affected through these industrial wastes, that drain into these water bodies.

Pathogenic microbes, parasites and other health hazards can be spread to man through consumption of fish that have been exposed to sewage. Where raw sewage is fed to fish directly or indirectly by draining into the fish ponds or even in vicinity of the fish ponds, there is serious risk of infection as these sewage constitute pathogenic, saprophytic bacteria, viruses and parasites. Whenever such infections are detected by health authorities, the most likely thing is to shut down the pond to save humans from being affected. This is happening in many parts of Africa. Rivers, ponds, lakes, dams, reservoirs or even irrigation canals which are located below pit-latrines which drain down ward into the valley can contaminate these water bodies unnoticed. Much of the flow is underground and many, particularly those in Third World nations, cannot detect the danger. In many countries such as India,

Philippines, and some South Asiatic nations, use human excrements to feed fish in ponds. In

some cases, some excrements have been treated before they are fed to fish, but still lots of

bacteria and viruses are still embedded therein. In such cases where humans consume fish

which have been exposed to such sewage may get infected and sometimes not. But since we

do not understand when individuals will be affected, the best procedure would be to abandon

feeding or even fertilizing fish ponds with human sewage or treated night soil. These are

some of the problems which affect fish production in many Third World nations, Africa

included (Pillay, 1993).

As one travels along the road in Africa, mainly the secondary roads, one finds human

excrements all along the road. Toilets are constructed behind each homes in villages without

consideration of what these can do to the ponds, rivers, wells, reservoirs, dams or even

irrigation canals which are situated in valleys below. As it rains, the soil erosion carries all

these night soils in the valleys below. Apart from causing turbidity in water, these night soils

infect the water bodies with bacterials, viruses, some of which are very deadly in the human

body.

Many fish kills have been caused by tankers that frequent major harbors and spilling

oil in various seaports like Assab, Mombasa, Dar-es-Salaam and Port-bel on Lake Victoria in

Uganda. Some of the environmental problems can take place regardless whether the state of

industrialization or urbanization is existent or not. These could be referred to as biological

pollutions. Water borne pathogenic micro-organisms or excessive growth of weeds could be some of the biological pollutions that are bound to affect fish farming and aquaculture in general.

As production of crops and the development of industries continue to take place all over the continent, more and more problems are created. Although pollutants such as insecticides, molluscicides, piscicides and even petroleum can be used for protection of the cultured stocks, and use of wastes for nutrient supply, but still these chemicals are very disastrous to human health. In Africa, pollutants, as mentioned earlier, have not reached an alarming stage like in Europe, China, Korea and other Southeast Asiatic nations. But all the same they are still some of the problems that hinder fish farming development on the continent.

Refineries have been mentioned many times as a source of water pollutions. Apart from the accidental release of oil during handling of petroleum, those industries can discharge phenolic compounds, acid waters, ammonia cyanide, chromate, detergents, solids and heat, these pose great danger to aquaculture industry. There are several methods in which these pollutions can be prevented, but many times facilities that can be used, are lacking in most African nations. Because of the absence of the machineries and expertise, simple things such as these, can throw aquaculture industry to a halt.

A large number of countries from Algeria to Mozambique grow cotton. Egypt and Sudan are the largest producers of cotton in Africa. But cotton alone consumes 2,200 tons of DDT. In the near future the need may become about six times as high (FAO-ACMRR, 1972). Gamma-BHC is used against the capsid bug in cocoa production in Ghana, Nigeria, Ivory Coast, and Cameroon. Fungicides, DDT, and Lindane are used a great deal in coffee production in Ivory Coast, Uganda, Kenya, and Zaire. All those pollutants are carried by rain

to ponds, rivers, lakes, dams, reservoirs, irrigation canals and these water bodies are

contaminated; and as a result fish production is affected.

In Egypt fish are killed frequently in small canals and Lake Quarun as a result of air

spraying, discarded cans and careless washing of contaminated clothes. Such bodies of water

like Lake Nasser, irrigation canals, dams, and the great water bodies of the Mediterranean Sea

are contaminated by the pesticides in the country. George also reported in 1972 that

pesticides have been equally damaging in countries like Sudan, Libya, Algeria and other

surrounding nations.

In some countries of Africa such as Uganda, Tanzania, Mozambique and Malagasy

Republic, rice crop could be very important. Much could be gained by expanding fish culture

in these rice paddies, using practices that have been witnessed in Asian countries like Taiwan,

China, South Korea and Philippines. In these countries, particularly the first three mentioned

above, agriculture including aquaculture has been given priority, but yet pesticides have been

used to the maximum. This has resulted into damages to fisheries. Agriculture in some

countries of Africa cannot survive without the use of pesticides and if agriculture is to thrive

then pesticides have to continue, but fisheries will have to cease because the rain and air will

deliver these chemicals to rivers, dams, ponds, irrigation canals, wells, and artificial lakes. By

the way, it must be understood that these chemicals are not only destructive to fisheries but to

human beings too.

In the Rift Valley and the Lake Victoria basin, there is an important cotton production

and drainage of pesticides from these regions to fish ponds, rivers and lakes is causing lots of problems in the region. In Cameroon, Egypt, and Malagasy Republic in Dakahlia district, the problem of insecticides is rampant because farmers need higher yields from their crops, thus increasing the problem of these pollutants (FAO-ACMRR, 1985).

Herbicides used to control aquatic weeds and fenoxyacetic acids are among the most common and probably the most toxic to fish. This is mainly so because of the impurities they contain. There is evidence that 2,4-D which is used very frequently can cause increased toxicity of insecticides. The effect is, however, reduced by suspended silt.

Many inorganic elements are metals that have great ecological effect. The most important metals are mercury, lead, cadmium, chromium, zinc and selenium. Mercury accumulates in aquatic organisms including fish and shellfish, and it has high toxicity in mammals. Methyl mercury is the most toxic mercurial compound. The normal levels of mercury in fish range between 0.01 and 0.2 ppm. Thus mercury as toxic metal leads to hazards of man's health.

Heavy metal like mercury appear in many different kinds of industrial wastes, and in municipal sewage waters like those found in city sewages all over Africa. Although, all African cities are exposed to this danger, yet no alarming reports have been provided regarding these heavy metals in fish or water. This could probably be due to lack of expertise needed to conduct the analysis of the water resources.

There is much room for argument in respect to pollutions in African fisheries, but one thing we must expect is that these pollutants are here to stay and they keep on increasing in toxicity as time goes on. If we want to acquire good successful aquaculture, good management is essential and can only come through educating nationals regarding aquaculture in Africa.

African Aquaculture

Aquaculture, as it is understood in Africa, means the art of introducing fish in lakes, rivers, dams, reservoirs and ponds. This is intended to promote fish species introduced in different parts of Africa from Europe and North America. These include species such as *Salmonidae, American brook trout, Salvelinus fontinalis*, Centrarchidae like (*Micropterus salmoides*, the *large-mouth black bass*) Cyprinidae as of the *European carp (Cyprinus carpio)*. Other indigenous species in Africa were stocked in waters in which they were non-endemic.

There are many reasons cited for introducing these exotic species in African aquatic environments, and African indigenous species in areas in which they are foreign: (1) Indigenous species in some large African waters have not adequately colonized the environments in which sufficient profits could be generated to sustain fish farming ventures in those environments. This can easily be corrected by selecting species which can grow well in certain environments at low costs. These species could be exotic or indigenous. If these species have been tested and found appropriate, then they could be exploited at a large scale in which case large profits could be generated. The government should make sure that rural farmers benefit from these profits generated from their labor. This will motivate and inspire them to work even harder and fish farming as such will be sustainable. This has been tried at Lake Tanganyika Chipeids, *Limnothrissa species* and *Stolothrissa spp.* in Lake Malawi. Introduction *Stolothrissa spp.* were made available into Lake Kivu, but were unsuccessful.

Other predatory species, such as *Lates niloticus*, or *M. salmoides*, are used to control prolific breeding species, but when these predators are given abundant food supply they become the commercial mainstay. When the endemic species are economically favorable, then the predator is introduced to control excessive fry and fingerlings which are vulnerable to predation. Some species are introduced in African water as instruments of biological control of aquatic vegetation, and can be used in situations where both rooted and floating vegetation are detrimental to fish life.

Fish culture development was successful in South and Central Africa, the Congo Basin, Cameroon, Nigeria, Egypt and Sudan, but nowhere in Afridca is fish farming as significant in contributing to protein diet of the population as it is in Far East and other tropical Asian countries.

Environmental Constraints

Temperature is one of the environmental factors that are significant in determining species for a pond culture. Some fish species cannot spawn unless certain limits of temperatures are available. *Tilapia mossambica* cannot do well in low temperatures. The right temperatures should be between 20° and 35°C (Chimits, 1955). *T. mossambica*, due to its ability to survive in relatively higher temperature than the three native species, namely *T. nilotica, T. galilea,* and *T. zillii*, would be preferred specie for culture, but it experiences a lot of mortalities in low temperatures, and this limits its productivity.

The European carp, *(C. carpio)*, has been cultured in Asia, Far East and South Africa, but this specie has not been successful in equatorial African regions. It is possible that environmental conditions within the tropics are inappropriate for this specie. The high

temperatures in these regions could affect the fertility of this specie or the ability of the young

one to mature (FAO, 1985).

American brook trout survived in cold waters in Kenya, but could not spawn due to

the fact that they had no gravel spawning grounds. But since they spawn in lakes in Sweden

without the gravel spawning grounds, it probably was not the reason for their inability to

spawn in equatorial African waters. The reason could have been turbidity, heavy metals and

other domestic wastes which drain into tropical ponds, dams, rivers and lakes as a result of

tropical rain pours. On the other hand, Someren and Whitehead stated that the male *T. nigra*

at Sagaua fish ponds in Kenya, had varied growth from month to month due to changing

environmental conditions. The most important ones are water temperatures rise and fall a few

degrees causing marked increases or decreases in body weight achieved (Okorie, 1960).

In tropical Africa, fish ponds get their water supplies from surface run-offs. These soil

erosion carry with it tons and tons of dissolved sediments. These drain into rivers, dams, fish

ponds, and irrigation canals. High turbidity due to suspended clay particles will be the result

of this heavy rainfall. The surface run-offs have become a permanent phenomenon in most

African waters and fish ponds. Turbidity affects the growth of certain fish in fish ponds.

High turbidity of water can affect productivity and fish life. It will reduce light penetration

into the water and thus decrease primary production. Oxygen deficiency has also been

reported as a result of a sudden increase in turbidity. The gills of fish may be injured by

turbid water. The effect will depend on the species and the nature of the suspended matter.

Turbid water in hatcheries should be avoided as it can greatly affect the hatching and rearing of larvae (Pillay, 1993).

In clear ponds with average turbidities of less than 25 ppm is about 1.7 times that of fish ponds of intermediate turbidities ranging from 25 to 100 ppm and is about 5.5 times greater than of a muddy fish pond whose turbidity is 100 ppm. Some species such as *large mouth bass* and *M. salmoides*, the latter one is the most adversely affected by high turbidity.

One of the outstanding limiting factors to aquaculture in Africa is the problem of regulating the breeding capacity of cultivated species, whether exotic or indigenous to African freshwaters. There are species that do not spawn naturally, there is need to induce them. A good example of such species are the *European Common Carp* and *C. carpio*. But there are species that breed in African waters very profusely. There is a need to control such breed. *Tilapia species* are the best example. In controlling the breeding, the spawners are placed at the right time and if the atmospheric conditions are favorable they will then spawn rapidly. The fry hatch out very fast and are gathered, counted and transferred to rearing ponds. This method is very good for carp (Huet, 1986).

With *Tilapia* species reproduction can be controlled through the association of tilapias with a predator. The predator will control the excessive undesired reproduction of *tilapias*. This has been tried with *Hemichromis fasciatus* in Zaire and Cameroon, *Lates niloticus* in Nigeria and with *Michropterus salmoides* in Madagascar or Malagasy Republic as it is called today (Huet, 1986).

Tilapia breeding can also be controlled by using "monosex cultivation." The ponds are stocked with species of one sex only. Male tilapias grow faster than females and two methods are possible side by side. The fish are observed and the two types of sex are

separated and are allowed to grow separately. This method is rather difficult, one needs to be

careful in separating the species. Mistakes can easily be made while separating them.

Hybridization has been used in Malaya. This was done by hybridization of *T. mossambica*

and *T. hornorum* from Zanzibar (Huet, 1986). *Carps* have done very well in lower and

middle latitude rivers in South Africa, Zimbabwe, and Malagasy Republic where

environmental conditions are similar to those in Jordan valley in Israel where *carps* have done

very well (Huet, 1986).

Carp culture in Africa demands a tougher measure of predator control, than otherwise

would have been in Europe, Far East for such predators like water beetles, tilapia fry,

fingerlings and frogs. *Rana* sp. and *Xenopus* sp. of frogs cause untold damages to *carps*.

Some scientists argue that given favorable environmental conditions, *carps* can reproduce

better than Tilapia species, in some parts of Africa. *Carps* in Asia and in the Far East are

doing extremely well in rural agricultural economy. This has been achieved not only by

availability of natural breeding stock, but also by perfecting the induced spawning techniques

(Akorie, 1972).

Bard (1960) noted that *M. salmoides* reproduce and grow fairly well in natural lakes,

but would not breed in ponds whose depth is never deeper than 2.5 M. *Black bass* prefer the

cooler waters of the lake than they would prefer the warm shallow ponds of Africa.

Oil and Petroleum Pollutants

Pollution by oil and petroleum and their byproducts have affected coastal harbors and industries greatly. The East African cities along the coast of Africa noted considerable increase of onshore pollutions by oil and tar from tankers which were stationed in the channel when Suez Canal was closed down temporarily. When the canal was opened, it reduced the pollution because most of the tankers moved away.

Oil residue have been shown to affect aquatic life in several ways, like altering bottom structure, smothering of fixed epifauna and plants and reduction of light penetration. When fish inhale oil and tar, an unpleasant flavor is acquired that renders fish unmarketable. If fish take in oil and tar they will usually die after a short time.

There are dispersants which can be used to remove the oil, but many government experts have written much against the use of dispersant that they cause more harm than good. They are considered more damaging in the near-shore and littoral zone, except under special circumstances. Less and less toxic dispersants have been developed and may be preferred to use a suitable dispersant against oil outside the coast rather than to ignore it and let it come onshore.

Biological Effects

The incidence of predation within natural or cultured fish population is more common in African freshwater systems than is perhaps experienced elsewhere. This implies that the fish to be cultivated should not only be given sufficient food supply within the aquatic environment, but should also be provided with protection from predation by other fishes, frogs, tadpoles, and aquatic birds.

Carp culture in the African environment demands a tougher strategy of predator control than otherwise would be needed in Europe or in the Far East. Predators such as water beetles, tilapia fry, fingerlings and frogs do untold damage to *carp* eggs and fry. In Jos and Nigeria fish farms, it was estimated that about 50% mortality rate result from predator activities (Fed. Fish Service, 1963).

The one outstanding limiting factors to aquaculture in the African environment has been the problem of regulating the breeding capacity of the cultivated species, exotic or indigenous to African freshwaters. This can be regulated by repressing breeding in those species with prolific breeding habits. This applies to the *tilapia species* (Cichilids). The breeding of these species has to be repressed otherwise this will inhibit growth and increase in size of fish cultivated.

Carp culture has succeeded in some parts of South Africa, Zimbabwe, and Malagasy Republic where climatic conditions are similar to those in Jordan valley in Israel where fish pond production is 5000 kg/ha/year is recorded. It is expected that given favorable conditions, production of *carp* in ponds can be better than that of *tilapia* in some parts of Africa. *Carp* culture in the Far East and Asia has been raised to such a level of proficiency that it is very significant in the rural agricultural economy. This has been so because it has been perfected by using induced spawning techniques (Okorie, 1966).

Lates niloticus would have been another desirable species for pond culture, but it has a high oxygen demand and is adversely affected by silty flood water which enter its environment, and yet oxygen deficiency and high turbidity are common characteristics of most African fish ponds.

The Human Factors

The environments have placed limitations on the African fish farmers on their capacity to produce cultured species in the aquatic environment and also on the economic returns from such ventures. In Africa, fish ponds, dams, and man made lakes are sources of health hazards to the human population in their vicinity (the *Anopheles*). The role of fish ponds seems to be merely the spread of malaria (*A. gambiae* and *A. funestus)* and the economic returns generated from such ponds is almost nil. It is no wonder therefore that many farmers would choose to avoid participating in fish farming and eliminate malaria from their vicinity. It is true that there may be other water bodies that would act as vectors for malaria such as rivers, lakes, dams, but if fish ponds are spread everywhere in the community, malaria will be much more spread than it would have been without them. This is one of the major limiting factors to fish farming in Africa. It is important, however, to realize that governments can and should fight against the spread of malaria all over the continent.

United States of America is a big nation, but through declaring war against malaria, this menace was completely eliminated from the country. If one country can do it within its borders, another country can do it too. Many leaders will give excuses that they do not have the money to fight this war. But many of these people borrow millions of dollars to buy military hardware to destroy their own people. In this same fashion they can borrow in an attempt to eliminate the menace of malaria. This will in return improve the production of fish

farming and eventually the economy will improve.

Bard, in the 1960's, reports that individuals who lived around fish ponds in the

Yaounde area in Cameroon had a problem of intestinal bilharziasis from the *Schistoma*

mansoni which is spread by *Biomphalaria camerunensis* (molluscs; planorbis) which are

abundant in ponds. *Bilharziasis* poses a big threat to fish breeding in Africa. In Ghana, as it

is in many parts of the Continent, Obeung (1966) reports that around Volta Lake encourages

the growth of molluscs, *Bulinus forskalii* and *B. rholfsi*, both of which act as intermediate

hosts of *vesical schistosomiasis*. This disease is very debilitating to humans which can easily

frustrate fish farming in areas where it is widespread. Many times questions are asked

whether the economic returns generated from the fish ponds warrant this human suffering.

The misuse of land resources in Africa in pursuit of technological innovations has led

to loss of useful landscapes and aquatic environments on the continent. One good example

can be found in Lake Baringo basin in Kenya, where commercial fish stocks are depleted due

to deterioration of water quality through silting, and by introduction of exotic species which

were meant to replenish the diminishing stock. These exotic species have been confronted

with hostile environmental systems too.

In Asia and the Far East where fish farming has attained significance in the rural

economy, supplemental feeding in fish ponds is given special emphasis. In Africa, on the

other hand, rural fish farmers do not, many times, use supplemental feeding. This leads to

poor yields and subsequent loss of interest by the fish farmers. This is basically due to the

integration of fish farming with other farming systems. Fish farmers do not give priority to fish farming per se, as they have many other things to do in other farming systems. If they only did fish farming, they would probably have given greater emphasis to it.

Artificial feeds are recommended to rural fish farmers. This includes cereals such as rice-bran, brewer's wastes, dried or fresh slaughterhouse wastes, and oil cakes. Some people do argue that African rural fish farmers may grow rice, but may not have the bran. It should be noted that breweries, rice, oil mills and abattoirs are located at industrial urban areas far away from the rural fish farmers. Artificial feeding may be good and appropriate for fish farming, but rural fish farmers in Africa may not be in a position to use it because they cannot get access to them. These are some of the major technical limiting factors to aquaculture on the continent, but there are other social factors to which we need to focus at this juncture.

Social Constraints

There is a lack of proper communication among African fish farmers. Kigeya (1995) reports that most of the farmers state that they get help from their respective fish farming officials. A few of the farmers say that they have their own social organizations through which they communicate to one another. Most farmers say that they have opportunity to visit and exchange ideas with their fellow farmers. Farmers have more relevant information than what they would get from magazines, journals, periodicals and newspapers. Farmers who live close together meet to discuss problems and new practices pertaining to fish farming.

Fish farmers in Uganda say that they still have a lot to learn. It is true they have enough fisheries officers and extension agents to advise them about fish farming, but still fish farming requires a lot more information and a lot more communication amongst fish farmers themselves. According to Kigeya, there is no communications among fish farmers in Uganda yet as each farmer is on his or her own. If fish farming is to become a commercial venture, then farmers should work as a team. They should exchange ideas, visit each other's farm, and be taken around on fish farms to learn new practices which one farmer might have not yet come across. Farmers also need additional information through reading newspapers, magazines, periodicals, journals as they need to learn more about fish farming than what they know now.

Fish eating is unpopular in some parts of Africa. In Bunyoro, Ankole, Kigezi and Karamoja, fish eating is rather unpopular. The people in these regions and probably many other regions elsewhere on the continent feel that fish smells too much. Some people who possess cattle have no need of fish when milk is around. In African traditions a rich man is the one with the greatest number of cows around. Such people despised all other professions, leave alone fishing. Fishing to them was one of the lowest jobs. These animal keepers depended on milk and meat. Fish were considered food for poor people, and people who depended on fish were categorized as poor and could not afford milk and meat which was food for most kings and the rich people. Thus this lack of eating of fish in these African communities implies that some people on the continent, despite the modernization, and the high technology, some Africans still think traditionally. Many of these people are highly educated. Most of them know how important fish farming is and yet through their traditions do not want to admit that they are depriving themselves of high biological food value proteins. It is, however, beginning to change since fish farming is being practiced in many of these regions and many people are getting exposed to these foods. This trend of thought is changing as more and more people from various parts of the continent mix up through churches, schools, intermarriages, and workplaces. The information which the non fish eaters get through mixing up is now changing their thinking as well as their eating habits (Kigeya, 1995).

Deforestation, overgrazing, and altered techniques in agriculture have increased erosion, significantly. This increases soil erosion and turbidity in fish ponds, dams, and any other aquatic reservoirs down below. Too many development projects have been developed following a relatively short on-site examination of the situation by outside planners who have never visited the area where a project was to be operated. Planners have rarely consulted the local people to find out what they consider to be their problems, needs, and priorities, and how they feel the project would best be implemented. But had the planners consulted carefully the local people, they would discover how people perceive their own needs and priorities. In a community lacking drinking water, for example, there is little point in starting any development project which does not deal with the water problem (Wakabi, 1993).

During the planning and implementation of many projects, nations, expatriates, specialists assigned to these projects should be educated to understand and also to accept local traditions, customs, and cultural views, all of which affect the responses of the local people to the ideas of change. This often results in indifference, suspicion and even hostility to such a change.

Educational Constraints

Educational problems can be many, but only a few are cited here below. Lack of qualified extension officers who are in constant touch with the farmers in rural areas, can hinder fish farming. In many African nations, the major constraints to the development of aquaculture is the scarcity of trained personnel, especially those with broad training and experience in the practical aspects of aquaculture production. There is need of trained personnel in areas such as senior aquaculturists, aquaculture technicians and extension workers (UNDP/FAO, 1975).

Most of the aquaculturists and aquaculturist technicians and extension workers should be trained in their own countries. The emphasis should be focused on appropriate production systems and the attending socio-economic conditions. Unfortunately this is not what happens and as such, many educated aquaculturists do not have appropriate practical experience. This hinders the development of aquaculture.

There are widespread problems of the structure and deployment of supposedly trained extension officers. Many developing countries maintain sizable services, numbering in some cases hundreds of extension staff. They are sometimes deployed in ones and twos in remote areas where they are expensive to maintain and difficult to support. Because of their dispersion, lack of specialized training, lack of equipment, transportation, or funds for day-to-day operation, support and supervision, lead to lack of effective execution of their responsibilities as expected. As farmers cannot come into contact with these extension staff, results into fish farming decline. Once extension agents are deployed, the government should be ready to get funds to support, maintain and even provide transportation to them so as to enable them to go to farmers to promote fish production.

In some developing countries, fisheries extension is made worse by the fact that extension agents are required to carry out lots of responsibilities such as collecting statistics, undertake licensing of fish crafts, collecting revenue, and enforcing regulations. Whoever undertakes to carry out these duties, he or she is suspected and disliked. The extension officers who carry out all these duties as stipulated cannot work with farmers effectively, because farmers won't trust him. Thus collective role of extension staff is direct implication that fish farming is declining, as there will not be friendly working relationship between extension agents and the farmers. Therefore an effective extension agent should deal only with extension work, as these other responsibilities will deter the success of his work (Kigeya, 1995).

Lack of proper understanding of fish farming in Africa has assisted in reducing the amount of fish production. If people have ever been exposed to fish marketing, they would find it impossible to accept the fact that fish farming in Africa can be turned into commercial ventures. This lack of proper information about fish farming on the continent impacts a great deal on how much the fish farmers can produce. It is significant that fish farmers be educated and trained in the skills they need to do decent fish farming activities which might eventually lead into commercial aquaculture programs. Proper training of fish farmers implies that people will be confident to take up fish farming because they will know what will be needed to make fish farming successful.

Fish farmers should be trained well by the extension agents, as this will increase their knowledge base regarding fish farming. Farmers need to be trained so as to diversify their fish farming. They should develop multiple types of aquaculture such as ornamental, dietary and sport fish farming. All these different branches of fish culture are significant in Asia, the Far East and in many places in Latin America. Fish farmers on the continent need to be informed that they should practice commercial fish culture. This would enable them to move from subsistence farming to commercial ventures, which the governments in various countries of Africa want the fish farmers to do in the 1990's.

Ineffective extension education impacts on the amount of fish the farmers can produce. The extension agents need to realize what is expected of them by the government. The main tasks for the fisheries extension agents can be defined as (a) transferring to fish farmers facts, information and technical know-how, new farming and fishing, fish handling and processing techniques and equipments; (b) informing and guiding fish farmers and thus enabling them to obtain credits and other financial assistance; (c) helping the fish farmers to organize themselves for better presentation of their views and interests and for rational utilization of available resources. Because the extension agents do not understand their responsibilities fully, they end up not carrying it out as expected. This makes the farmers participate in ventures which they do not fully understand. Thus the ultimate products are limited as a result of the limited information the farmers get from the extension agents.

Apart from the extension agents from whom the farmers receive fish farming information, farmers also need reading materials such as magazines, journals, periodicals and

books. Since fish farming information cannot be received only from fisheries officers,
farmers need to depend on publications for their current technical knowledge.

At the level of fish farming in Africa, the fish farmer might have enough source of
information, but if fish culture in Africa is changed from subsistence to commercial, more
current information will be necessary. At present, in some parts of the continent, particularly
the rural areas, communication among farmers is lacking. Each farmer is on his or her own.
But if this venture is to change, communication and working togetherness among fish farmers
is a must. Farmers themselves need to start writing about their own experiences in fish
farming. This will inspire other farmers to participate in aquaculture, after reading what other
farmers are going through and the good experience will motivate the on-lookers to take up the
venture.

Since some of the aquaculturists are well educated, who can put their ideas and
experiences on paper, these should be encouraged to write articles in newspapers, magazines,
journals and books. Those involved in fish farming need to learn to advertise their papers and
other local publications. Although aquaculture in Africa is not yet gone commercial, but with
all these reading materials and advertisements will improve the image of this venture and will
attract more and more people into it.

Encouraging fish farmers to participate in seminars, conferences, lectures and any
other discussion groups would help them to broaden their knowledge base in fish culture.
Communication is one of the factors that is very significant among fish farmers. If
communication is emphasized, it will result into fish farming promotion.

Summary

Problems that are hindrances to fish production in Africa are grouped into three different categories, namely: technical, social and educational. Technical problems outweigh the other two categories. Pond construction, maintenance, feeding fish in ponds, fertilizing of fish ponds, are some of the technical problems. Social problems such as lack of communication among fish farmers, lack of understanding of local traditions, lack of consultation between farmers and project initiators, lack of adequate transportation stand in way of fish farming. Educational problems like lack of trained extension agents, lack of proper communication among farmers, lack of reading materials such as magazines and newspapers are hindrances to fish production on the continent.

CHAPTER VI

CONTROL OF WEEDS, PESTS, AND PREDATORS

In this chapter, various aquatic plants and how to control them will be discussed. Pests and predator control will be dealt with next. Summary will be compiled at the end of the chapter.

Aquatic plants and weeds in various aquaculture farms are problems in different regions of the world. These plants and weeds are more problematic in tropical and semi-tropical fish ponds and mainly in undrainable ponds (Pillay, 1993). If plant growth is limited may be good in maintaining water quality and can serve as food organisms in water.

Uncontrolled plant growth affects fish farming operations. Sometimes fish movements are restricted, dense growths of vegetation like the floating plants stand in the way of light penetration into the water and eventually prevents productivity. Photosynthesis and oxygen production will be cut short if the water surface is covered with plants and weeds. This reduces oxygen to cultivated fish and causes anoxia to those animals. A lot of nutrients in the water and those put in water through fertilization will be used up by weeds and plants in water. This will reduce the production of cultivated animals.

The blooming of algae and other aquatic plants leads to oxygen depletion as a result of dead and decaying algae mass (Huet, 1986).

Phytoplankton

The phytoplankton of a small farm such as small ponds, dams, reservoirs will usually consist of microscopic plants which are suspended in the water body. Some of these aquatic species are mobile and some can only move by water current and turbulence of water by the wind. When there is abundance of phytoplankton in the water, the water color will change, sometimes to green, red, yellow, brown, black, gray or various other colors.

Most varieties of phytoplankton move and separate easily. The species of phytoplankton which occupy certain locations depend on the habitat for the growth of the individual species (Boyd, 1990). Phytoplankton require at least one percent of sunlight for proper growth. Too much sunlight can inhibit growth for certain species. Aquaculture ponds are infested with various types of phytoplankton. Some ponds contain too much turbidity that sunlight cannot penetrate through the water. By so doing phytoplankton is inhibited from growth. When phosphorus is added to the water, plant growth is increased. Phytoplankton productivity may be regulated by growth of macrophytes because these plants compete with phytoplankton for food in water.

Macrophytes

The growth of macrophytes increase when there is increment of nitrogen and phosphorous also with increasing alkalinity. Turbidity as in case of phytoplankton, limits the growth of macrophytes. Macrophytes are usually absent in waters which have moderate to heavy plankton blooms. As phytoplankton increases in concentration in water, the more will macrophytic algae reduce from that water body. In the same way when macrophytes are abundant in the water, phytoplankton withdraws from that same environment (Boyd, 1990).

According to Pillay (1993), aquatic weeds can best be classified according to their habits and habitat. Some common types are as follows:

Common Aquatic Weeds:

1. Floating weeds: These float around and on top of the water surface. The roots are under the water and the leaves above the water surface. Good examples are *Eichhornia, Pistia,* and *Azolla.*

2. Emergency weeds: These have their roots deep down at the bottom soil of the pond, but leaves are above the water surface. Examples are *Nyphaea, Trapa,* and *Myriophyllum.*

3. Plankton algae: This is free floating cells of single or colonial habit, forming characteristic groups, short strands, or spheres with or without power of movement, e.g. *Phacus, Scenedesmus, microcystis* and *pandorina.*

4. Filamentous algae: Usually from strands of threads of cells that may grow on pond bottom but float to the surface forming scums or floating mats of hairlike strands, e.g. *spirogyra* and *zygnema.*

5. Algae that grow upward from the pond bottom in a plant form not unlike that of some of the higher plants like *Nitella* and *Chara.*

Tilt Deck Trailer.

onveyor combination,

Standard Trailer,

SHORE CONVEYOR

Trailer-Conveyor

The higher plants can be divided into:

(a) Floating aquatic plants: These are unattached, and they float about on the surface
    of the waters; water hyacinth (*Eichonia*), watermeal (*Wolffia*), duckweed (*Lemna*),
    mosquito fern (*Azolla*) (Bennett, 1971).

(b) Submerged aquatic plants: These are found mostly below the surface and
    supported mostly by water: pond weeds (*potamogeton*), coontail (*Ceratophylum*),
    water weeds (*Elodea*), milfoil (*Myriophyllum*).

(c) Emergent rooted aquatic plants: These are found mostly above the surface and
    are self-supporting: cattails (*Typha*), bulrush (*Scirpus*), arrowheads (*Sagittaria*).

(d) Woody plants and trees: not really true aquatic but are usually associated with
    water: button bush (*cephalanthus*), cypress (*Taxodium*), willows (*Salix*).

(e) Marginal weeds: These fringe the shoreline of the waterbody and are usually
    rooted in water-logged soils such as (*Typha, phragmites*).

These plants, as discussed above, serve a lot of purposes in the water. Some act like
sources of food to some aquatic herbivorous organisms, some serve as a substrata on which
some animals hide, but again some of these plants serve as covers and mechanical aids for the
animals to escape from the innumerable natural predators that are found everywhere in the
water.

The aquatic plants are much unstable unlike the terrestrial environments. This is true
in terms of algae, which are short lived and very sensitive to minute changes in the
environments, and the submerged aquatic plants which may be shaded out by turbid water
(Bennett, 1971).

<u>Various Types of Algae and Aquatic Weeds</u>:

(i)   Algae for oxygen production: Plankton, a type of algae liberates oxygen and it is dissolved in the water around. This is the basic source of dissolved oxygen in water during winter.

(ii)   Algae as basic food: Some types of algae function as basic food for the herbivorous organisms in the water. In this case some of these algae species are more valuable than others. But at this juncture, very little is understood about specific aquatic food chains and the various species of algae (Bennett, 1971). Plant cells and plant debris function as food for certain aquatic animals like protozoa to fishes. It is stated clearly in various sources that fishes that are important for angling are not herbivorous or eat only limited amounts of plants. Bluegills feed mainly on insect larva and Entomostraca, yet in some seasons it feeds on algae and leaves of some aquatic weeds.

(iii)   Dangerous algae: Many species of *blue-green algae* produce toxic substance when they die and decay. These algae have been the cause of death for *mammalian, avian,* and *fish*. These algae are dangerous when they appear on the lakes and ponds and scattered abroad by wind along the lake margins. The people who drink such water and the blue-green algae cells are poisoned.

(iv)   Nuisance algae: Most *filamentous algae* are considered nuisance plants because they usually rise to the water surface. They float as green slime or scum. They disintegrate when they die and even at this time they are still dangerous to swimmers, and foul motor blades, boaters, and fishermen.

There are several types of *filamentous algae* that grow luxuriantly on the pond or lake surface to form a thick blanket that may completely cover the pond. Lawrence cites *Pithophora* as a nuisance form of algae; Hansen et al. describes a pond in southern Illinois that was nearly covered with floating layer of *Rhizoclonium*; and Hatchery personnel in the northern states are sometimes bothered with *Hydrodictyon*, a type of algae in which the elongated cells are arranged in the form of a net with six sided mesh. Small fish become entangled in these algae nets because they cannot escape (Bennett, 1971).

(v)   Water hyacinth (*Eichonia*) is the most known floating weed. It does not only cover aquaculture farms but also all other types of water bodies in Asia, Africa, Latin America, and other parts of the world. It spreads so fast that it can increase 700 percent in 50 days. It has covered many parts of Lake Victoria, at Luzira, Gaba, Jinja Owen Falls Dam, many parts of Albert-Nile, Kyoga, many other parts in Kenya, and Tanzania.

There are other floating weeds which are also as fast in spreading as water hyacinth (*Eichonia*). These are Pistia (*water lettuce*), Salvania, which grow very fast and cover large areas of aquaculture farms and other open water bodies. *Lamna* (duck weed) can grow in a very short time and cover a large area.

(vi)   Some submerged weeds are generally more difficult to control. Weeds such as *Hydrilla, Najas, Nitella, Vallisneria, Potamogeton, Ceratophyllum, Utriculeria,* and *Chara* are some of the most difficult submerged weeds to eradicate.

(vii)   There are some of the emergent weeds, such as *Nymphaea, Nelumbium, Trapa* and

Myriophyllum, which can easily be controlled.

(viii) Many marginal weeds are undesirable in many parts of the world, but Eastern

European nations, a reed belt is preserved in large fish ponds to control wave actions.

Phragmites and *Typha* are the two common marginal weeds used as wave controllers.

Methods of Weed Control

To prevent infestation of weeds in your aquaculture farm is to be careful to avoid

shallow areas around the margins of your pond. The pond depth at the margin should be

between .75 m to .9 m. This will prevent possibility of offshore weeds from entering the

pond. These are the ones that become a nuisance in our aquaculture farms. Accumulation of

silt in the pond can be prevented by stopping run-offs from entering your pond. It will also

be good to desilt your ponds annually and erecting barriers or mesh filters to prevent entry of

nuisance weeds, their spores or seeds.

All the methods can be used but many do not completely stop the entry of noxious

weeds into your aquaculture farm. To be sure that dangerous weeds are prevented the four

methods must be used to eliminate the weeds. You can use one method of the four or you

can combine any two methods or more to ensure complete elimination of these nuisance

weeds. The four methods are: (1) manual, (2) mechanical, (3) chemical, or (4) biological

(Pillay, 1993). The type of the method to be used will depend on the nature of the

infestation, the nature of the farm and the species of animals that are cultured.

Created from a need to knock down weeds so that clean ice could be cut from frozen lakes, Harvesters have  evolved greatly in the last several decades. Through research and development, we have taken the Aquatic Plant Harvester from its crude and cumbersome  origins to the efficient machines available today. By cutting and removing aquatic vegetation, harvesting offers an  environmentally sound, cost effective and practical solution to controlling excessive plant growth. A full range of sizes are available to suit every application.

TRASH HUNTERS

SWAMP DEVIL AQUATIC WEED CUTTER

AMPHIBIOUS DREDGE

It is also important to select the appropriate time to control these weeds. It is important to take control measures at the most vulnerable period in the life history of the weed (Pillay, 1993). Thus the best time to treat water hyacinth is during its vegetative growth when it is very susceptible.

The cost is another factor that should be considered when choosing the method to use in treating any weed; it also depends on country and location where the method is going to be put into practice. The cost of initial treatment and that of the subsequent treatments. By combining the methods such as manual and chemical, we can bring down the costs. The cost of weed control can be brought down if some weeds can be put to productive use. Some of the aquatic weeds can be converted to food, fertilizers, paper, fibre and energy (Pillay, 1993).

The two most convenient ways weeds can be put to use are (1) by using it as fertilizers and (2) as fodder for herbivorous aquatic animals. The weeds are harvested and spread out in the sun and after one day or two, be put into a compost manure. The heat that is retained through composting results into multiplication of microorganisms which will digest or break down those weeds into smaller particles.

Manual and Mechanical Methods

In small ponds, dams, lakes and water reservoirs, it is possible to remove floating weeds manually. We can use just simple tools such as hand scythes, wire mesh, coir nets, etc. Weeds such as water hyacinth, arrowhead (*sagittaria*), *water lettuce, Salvinia, duck weeds, Azolla, Spirodella,* and *Hygrorhiza* are examples of floating weeds which can be removed from an aquaculture farm using these simple tools. It is sometimes difficult to eradicate the floating weeds completely from ponds, but repeated removal together with biological or chemical methods may keep the weeds under control.

Some types of mechanical equipment have been devised for weed control. Some of these were meant for large bodies of water such as lakes and very large ponds, then some of the mechanical devises can only be used in large aquaculture farms.

Weed cutter is the commonest device that can be used on large farms. There are several weed cutters: Some have flat bottoms which have been fitted with cutting beams or other cutting devices with two cutting beams--one beam horizontal and the other vertical. Some motor-propelled boats fitted in front with two circular cutting beams, one beam is vertical and the other horizontal (Pillay, 1993).

Weed cutting should be frequently done so as to keep weed growth under check. Two to four times per annum should be done. In tropical regions cutting should be done as often as possible to keep the weeds in control.

Chemical Methods

Treatment of weeds with chemicals show relatively rapid results. The chemical is also detrimental to the cultured animals. The amount of concentration of chemicals will definitely affect species in the water. It will, however, destroy the weeds rapidly and the accumulation of the dead weeds will be very problematic. These weeds can be removed manually or mechanically. If they are left there to decay, they will create oxygen depletion in the water. On the other hand, the nutrients released by disintegrated weeds will add to the fertility of the farm and lead to further growth of the weeds.

The growth of weeds will affect the growth of phytoplankton which would be very essential to the cultured species.

Pillay (1993) in his book recommends the use of inorganic fertilizer will encourage the growth of phytoplankton which will cover the water surface and prevent the growth of the nuisance weeds. This method has been criticized in the tropics where the water is already fertile, to add another fertilizer will only encourage the growth of weeds rather than the phytoplankton.

The chemicals are applied on the leaves of the weeds in the water. In case of rooted vegetation, chemicals are applied on the soil through which the roots penetrate. Some chemicals select particular weeds to eliminate, but others do not.

The effectiveness of the chemicals will depend on types of weeds, the time, the method used to destroy the weeds, and the nature of the water body. This chemical treatment must be accompanied with manual or mechanical removal of weeds as well as effective farm management. Many countries in the world prohibit the use of chemicals in waters of aquaculture farms.

Among the herbicides, 2,4-D (*2,4-dichlorophenoxy acetate*) has been used widely in controlling the floating and emergent weeds by foliate application. It is commercially available as an acid, sodium salts, amine salts, or as esters (Pillay, 1993).

The amines and esters have been widely used in controlling the *water hyacinth*. *Pistia, Myriophyllum, Inula* and *Prosopsis* can be used to eradicate water hyacinth by spraying it at one percent aqueous solution. Diquet *(6,7,dihydrodipyrido* (1,2-a:2', 1'-c) pyrazidiinium salt) is easy to apply in pond farms. They are reported to be effective against emergent, floating, and submerged weeds. If waterbody has a lot of suspended particles these chemicals' effectiveness is reduced. In which case, these chemicals should be used in clear waters (Pillay, 1993).

Copper sulphate (CuSO₄) is the most widely and economical weedicide in algae control. 1-3 ppm of Copper Sulphate Pentahydrate (CSP) is said to be most effective for several algae. Anhydrous ammonia is used to eradicate submerged weeds like the *Hydrilla* and *Najas*. Ammonia acts quickly and does not leave residual toxicity. It is also possible to save the cultured species if treatment is done in sections. Ammonia treatment is time consuming and expensive, but would serve as nutrient in the water.

The recommended dose of ammonia for the eradication of submerged weeds is 12 ppmN and the gas is applied from a cylinder at a speed of 217 kg per hour. The weeds die within five days.

Biological Control

Herbivorous animals: The most important biological methods used in fish culture are herbivorous animals or fertilization. Principally fish that feed on plants only are very rare. But the main species are grass carp (*Ctenopharyngodon idella*) from China and the herbivorous tilapia (tilapia vendalli), and *Melanopleura (Tilapia zillii)*. These are warm water species and cannot eradicate the aquatic vegetation unless the temperature is above 20°C. Grass carp can resist winters while *Tilapia rendallii* die quickly when temperatures go below 12-13°C. These fish species' use is limited within tropical or hot temperate regions.

If this is not done, these higher plants will be stimulated into growth. The climatic conditions of the place will also play a big role in making this method successful.

More effective and delicate is the use of organic manure: dung, compost, and liquid manures. Some ponds of *cyprinid species* are supplied with water containing organic matter. By using this method, sewage water is purified but its use needs mixing polluted and fresh water as well as regular control. There will be a danger of disease and lack of oxygen.

Predators, Weed Animals and Pests Control

Predators and pests are not given significance in aquaculture, but yet the damage they cause is significant. Pelican can consume one to three tons of fish a year, ten pair of cormorants catch about 4.5 tons of fish in a year. Herons may destroy 30 to 40 percent of the fry in a pond farm. One heron may consume as many as 100 kg of fish in a year. Bird predators are known to have destroyed as many as 75 percent of fish production in Texas (Pillay, 1993).

Otters can destroy as much as 80 percent of the farm production. Usually they kill but do not eat all that they kill. The measures that are taken are partially effective as predatory birds and animals find ways of circumventing these control measures. Most of the pests in fish farms are difficult to control and they require constant application with considerable number of workers.

Grass carp species have been introduced to Russia, but the time is too short to determine whether they can be effective in eradication of aquatic vegetation, in other regions other than the tropical regions. *Herbivorous tilapia* survive on semi-submerged, floating and even on submerged part of emergent plants provided that they are not too tough.

The development of submerged and floating plants can be stopped indirectly by releasing a large number of 2- or 3-year-old carp. Four hundred carp weighing 250 gm are necessary. These carps as they search for food, dig into the bottom, stir up and cloud the water and stop the penetration of light and consequently the development of vegetation (Huet, 1983).

By using large number of fish, it is possible to eliminate lightly rooted plants. It is sometimes disappointing that occasionally in some ponds where grass carps are found, there are growth of *filamentous algae*. This is disappointing but very often *grass carps* eradicate the growth of floating plants.

Swans and ducks can also help control submerged plants when they look for food in those parts of the ponds which are shallow. *Nutria*, feed on emergent vegetation. Their cultivation is not widespread and the interest in them will depend on prices which can be received from their fur. Cattle can also eat emergent plants in shallow ponds (Huet, 1983).

Fertilization

Some fertilizers help the development of phytoplankton which obstructs light from penetrating into the water. This hinders the development of the higher plants. When fertilizers are to be used, floating, emergent and submergent vegetation must be removed first.

Predators

Predatory fish may get to aquaculture farms through water supply or through seeds brought into the farm. The water draining in preparation of new stock offers opportunities to the farmers to control some of the predatory fish. It is easy to control the spread of oil emulsions to prevent aerial breathing of insect larvae or fencing to prevent the entry of frogs.

Among birds, cormorants, fish eagles, herons, and kingfishers are considered the worst predators. Herons and egrets are the major predators in Texas shrimp ponds. Grobes, shore birds, and gulls are only looking for food and prey on shrimp when the water is low.

Several methods of controlling bird predators are used and some of them are as follows. For raceways and small ponds, can be covered with nets or wire mesh. But some birds learn how to go through these protective covers. Devices such as flash guns, sirens, klaxon horns, gongs, scarecrows, bamboo rattles, and bells have been used with varying successes. In Southeast Asian nursery ponds, farmers tie lines of strings on poles set in the pond and attach bright colored pieces of cloth or metal to the strings to scare birds. Sometimes windmill with mirrors that revolve and flash brilliantly are being utilized in Malaysia to scare birds. These devices can be used but accompanied by watchmen. But watching can be made difficult because birds such as herons are active mainly at night. Some of the fish eating birds are protected by the law, still some are shot or caught by spring traps. With some birds, they can be poisoned and nests destroyed (Pillay, 1993).

Frogs and toads are reported for destroying larvae and fish juveniles. Other predators are crocodiles, alligators and large lizards. All these can be protected by fencing the ponds and by keeping the pond banks around free from dense growths of vegetation.

Otters are the most destructive mammalian predators. These live close to the ponds and make holes in roots of trees. They do their most damage at night. They hunt for fish in clear nights mainly. They can be prevented by catching them with otter traps. The traps have to be strong and solid otherwise the otters will escape. Men are also among the fish poachers who are difficult to prevent. This problem is world wide and its seriousness varies from place to place. In several occasions, many types of burglar alarms and electrical fencing have been tried with varying success.

Weed Animals and Pests

Weed fish, that is species which fight for food with other cultured species, are to be removed. This can be achieved if done systematically. Weed fish gain access to aquaculture farms very early in the original incoming water. In aquaculture farms where open-water culture systems are practiced, elimination of weed fish is less expected. In the confined aquaculture waters, weed fish get access to ponds through the incoming water. By screening the water right from the initial entrance, the wild fish and other aquatic animals are eliminated or reduced to a large extent.

According to Pillay (1993), there are two types of filters used to catfish farms: a Saran sock filter and a box filter. Sock filter is cylindrical in shape, made by sewing together two pieces of Saran screen and provided with a draw-string closing arrangements at each end. The inlet pipe is placed inside one end of the filter and the draw-string is tied around it. The other end is also tightly tied to prevent escape of fish and other animals. The filter is cleared regularly to remove the dirt. Box filter may be made to float or fixed permanently below the inlet.

Most filters will not be able to prevent the entry of small organisms and eggs of weed species. Certain species of snails, mainly those of the family *Cerithidae* are major fighters for food in fresh and brackish waters when they occur in abundance. Large numbers of these species enter fish farms as larvae and grow and multiply rapidly. They affect the growth and abundance of algae in the water in Southeast Asia.

The ponds can be made muddy and the algae break up from the bottom and begin floating on the surface. The wind and wave push these floating algae to the bank where they decompose and produce large amounts of hydrogen sulphide. Very dense population of snails have been reported from coastal ponds in Indonesia (Pillay, 1993; Huet, 1983; Bennett, 1971).

Manual and mechanical removal of snails can also be effective if they are carried out after the ponds are drained. If the pond cannot be drained then one can use *Bayluscide (5,2-dichloro-4-nitro-salicylicaniline-ethanolamine)*, at a concentration of 3 ppm in the pond water, has been suggested. But Bayluscide has longer and other commercials have residual effects for varying periods of time (Pillay, 1993; Huet, 1983). Polychaete worms are serious pests in coastal ponds. They live at the bottom of the pond and loosen the soil allowing the water to escape. The growth of algae is also hindered. Crabs also affect the safety of the farm itself. Because the damage crabs cause to the aquaculture farms, farmers spend a lot of time trying to destroy them. Farmers use various trapping devices or chemicals to destroy these pests from the pond farms and their neighborhoods.

The burrowing shrimp (*Thalassina*) is another pest in certain areas where it destroys dikes, and they can be detected by the high mounds at the entrance of their holes. Muskrats and field rats both dig holes and high mounds are seen close to these holes. They also burrow in banks, dikes and in the end weaken the whole structure.

Regular cleaning and drying should be conducted to keep these structures in good conditions. Treated wood should be used in these structures to avoid decay. They can be painted with preservative paints that are not toxic to fish in the water. Cement should also be used to make structures to control the water.

Tea seed has wide use as a biocide in ponds and can be used to control snails and unwanted fish. One can apply it at 15-18 kilograms per one hectare (Lannan, 1986). Tobacco wastes are also used to control snails, polychaete worms and competitor and predator fish in Indo-Pacific ponds and African ponds. In tropical regions where tobacco is plentiful, it should be used more often to control pests and predators. From the derris plant, Raenone is widely used as a pesticide. The application of this pesticide varies from individual to individual. Hall (1949) advocates 0.5 ppm, Alikunki (1957) states that it should be 20 ppm. Quick lime can be applied in a pond after it has been drained and dried at 100 kilograms per hectare. Phenol is added to the pond surface after the pond is drained. It will control polychaete worms, even those that are buried in the mud. Endrin can be applied in a pond at 0.1 ppm according to Lannan, Smitherman, and Tchobanoglous (1986). Tadtox is also mentioned that it could be used to control tadpoles in the ponds in America (Lannan, 1986). Physical and chemical procedures are utilized in pond aquaculture farms. Physically the pond can be drained and dried before stocking and screening the inflow water. Some birds can be prevented from entering aquaculture farms by fencing off the ponds.

Sometimes collecting and removing unwanted snails is also effective in aquaculture ponds in Philippines and in Africa. Pond drying in conjunction with the use of chemical can be very beneficial in controlling snails.

Oysters, barnacles and *polychaete* worms that go through the screens and sluices in ponds can be effectively controlled by periodic drying and physical removal by hand (Lannan, 1986). Traps and other physical removal can be used effectively in controlling crabs and crustacean pests (Pillay, 1970). Toads in African ponds can be trapped and removed (Huet, 1972). Snakes can be controlled by trapping or can be killed by the workers of the facility and predatory birds and otters can be controlled by trapping or shooting (Lannan, 1983).

CHAPTER VII

FISH DISEASE, PUBLIC HEALTH CONSIDERATIONS

IN WARM WATER POND AQUACULTURE

This chapter is intended to discuss the consumer-related diseases, nonconsumer-related diseases, and fish diseases as they affect aquaculture industry.

Public Health Considerations in Warm Water Pond Aquaculture

Public health diseases in aquaculture farms are the diseases of animals which can be transmitted to man through aquaculture activities. These are diseases which can be categorized as those that affect the consumer and two, those which affect pond employees or people living close to aquaculture farms.

Diseases that Affect the Consumer:

Five bacterial diseases of man are: *Salmonellosis, shigellosis, vibriogastroenterities, botulism,* and *clostridium perfringens enterotoxemia* that have been associated with the consumer of the contaminated fish products (World Health Organization, 1968). Other diseases that result from consuming of pond raised *tilapia* are not documented as they should have been. Fish, particularly from freshwater, can be causatives to *metazoan parasites* that can affect man. Some of these are: (i) the broadfish tape worm (*Diphyllobothrium latum*). These can be found in some parts of Europe, Asia, Australia, North and South America, and

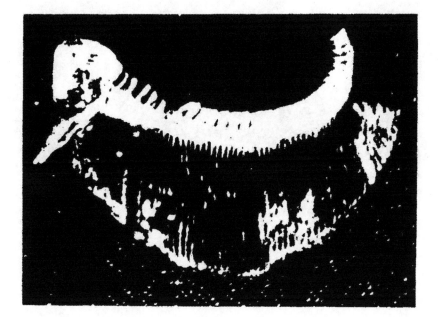

. Common Carp Gills Affected by Flexibacter Columnaris, a cause for Columnaris Disease. (Pillay, 1985).

Hand stripping of female fish. It is significant to make distinctive sex characteristics.

Many Species do not have these distinctive sex characteristics.

Barrage Type of Pond Farm

Africa. In other words, tape worms can be found everywhere in the world where freshwater fish is available (Healy & Juranate, 1979, in Lannan, 1986).

(ii) Flukes *Clonorchis sinensis, opisthorchis species*. These flukes parasites are common in Asia: China, Philippines, Malaysia, and Thailand, and in Africa in countries such as Uganda, Kenya, Tanzania, Zambia, Nigeria and in many other countries where people step in water bare-footed and where freshwater fish are available. Fish are actually secondary intermediate hosts for these parasites. The parasites harbor in some organ tissues of the fish, then humans who consume these infected fish are in return infected. This will be very frequent among people whose neighborhoods are dirty. If human excrements are scattered everywhere along the streets or if toilets are situated in locations where they are likely to contaminate the water bodies below, the surface run-offs will carry these domestic wastes, excrement and all unclean stuff around the neighborhoods into the fish ponds. The fish therein will consume these dirty materials.

In some countries such as China, India, and other nations where human excrements are used as fertilizers and feeds for the pond fish, human beings who feed on such fish will catch the diseases. In such environments *intestinal parasitism* is very prevalent. It is estimated that 3.5 million individuals in Thailand, China, Laos, and Vietnam are infested with these intestinal parasites. When the individual consumes improperly cooked or processed fish meat from water bodies which were contaminated with human excrements he or she may be affected (Lannan, 1986).

Nonconsumer-Related Diseases:

Leptospirosis is a bacterial disease of mammals transmitted through contact with urine of or water contaminated with *Leptospira*. This disease is found world wide. It is considered an occupational hazard of agricultural workers, abattoir and fish handlers, sewer workers, veterinarians and other people who are always in contact with domestic animals. Although pathogenic *Leptospira* from pond water used in fish culture the origin of which is now shown, but still Leptospirosis should be considered as a potential occupational diseases for aquacultural employees.

Schistosomiasis (Bilharzia):

Schistosomiasis is a severe parasitic disease which humans acquire through skin penetration by infective *cercaria* while the person is immersed in infested water. The human *schistosomiasis* is related to specific species of *snails* which are the intermediate hosts for the parasite. More than 100 million people are affected with this disease in Asia, Africa and Latin America (National Academy of Sciences, 1977).

If the water contains *snails*, then the contamination with human or animal wastes which contains *schistosome eggs*, constitutes a public health hazard. In controlling these hazards, proper disposal of sewage and animal wastes, *snails* control on water bodies should be conducted, prevention of contact with infective *cercaria* waters should be encouraged. In controlling snails, the grass that grows in or near the pond should be removed (Lannan et al., 1986). The stocking of species of fish that feed on mollusks to reduce the snails populations will be helpful. The appropriate species could be Black carp (*Mylophayngodon piceus*), African lung fish (*protopterus sp.*), Cichlids *serranochromis*, and many others. There should be periodic draining and drying out of the pond in conjunction with the application of the lime. There should be prevention of contamination of the pond by human and animal feces which might contain Schistosome eggs.

Malaria:

Anopheline mosquitoes are the major cause of malaria. This takes place mainly in slow running water which acts as a breeding ground. If the pond is well managed, malaria will not be a big problem there (Lannan et al., 1986).

In large ponds, the banks must be kept clear of grass and unshaded. The pond must be stocked by *larvae* eating fish and drained as soon as they are left unattended. Smaller ponds around the area are to be managed properly otherwise they will breed mosquitoes instead.

There are other types of mosquitoes which cause human malaria, are mainly transmitted by sixty various species of mosquitoes. The parasite is introduced into the human blood stream as *sporozoite* by the bite of an infective mosquito. In the human host, the parasite develops and multiplies, first in the liver, then in the blood stream, then it attacks the blood cells. When the *Anopheles mosquitoes* bite an infested human they carry the virus with them. When these mosquitoes bite other human beings they introduce the virus into another human blood stream and then the process is repeated. In controlling these mosquitoes, the aquatic farms should be managed in such a way that these other ponds do not become breeding grounds of these mosquitoes. Properly constructed pond farms with adequate drainage facilities will cut down the risks of malaria producing mosquitoes. When shallow ponds are constructed and remain covered with weeds and not properly managed in respect to drainage systems, they will equally be mosquito breeding grounds as the swamps on which

the ponds are built. The ponds should be 2 to 3 feet deep and the pond should be kept free

of all weeds. All floating and emergent weeds should be eliminated from the ponds. Animals

should be prevented from grazing around the pond as hoof prints are good breeding grounds

for mosquitoes. Many species of fish will feed on mosquitoes and thus they (mosquitoes) will

be reduced from the ponds (Pillay, 1993).

Fish Diseases

Bacterial Diseases:

Diseases of aquaculture caused by parasites and infectious diseases have attracted

attention of veterinarians and fish biologists for quite some time. With increasing investments

in aquaculture and closer examination of factors, health protection measures have developed in

recent times (Pillay, 1993).

Stress factors for fish in a pond will depend on frequent fluctuations in water

temperatures, water chemistry different from what the specie is used to, chemical substance,

polluted water, crowding, water saturated with human excrement, improper diet, transfers,

moving overly strong water circulation, and being kept in unsuitable ponds, and fish fear. All

these factors are contributive to pond fish stress. Frequent handling or netting, or even rapid

movement of the tank in which species are protected can trigger stress. Extreme stress can

lead to shock and death to the animal in the pond (Untergasser, 1990). Fish are usually

exposed to stress from the substances in the water. For some time, fish can maintain its homeostasis or body equilibrium by adapting to the changing factors. When fish are no

longer able to adjust, this ends up in death.

Overpopulation is equally dangerous to species cultured in the pond. Even with good

filtration, the water will still be polluted with waste products from these crowded fish species

(Untergasser, 1990).

Viral and Bacterial Diseases:

Viral Diseases: In Latin, the word virus means slime, juice, or poison, was for a long

time the general name for pathogen, but today the name virus is restricted to pathogenic

particles that are too small that they pass filters that hold bacteria. Virus consist of chemical

shell that contain genetic molecules (RNA). When the virus attaches itself to the wall of a

cell, will inject RNA into the cell. Then RNA becomes part of the cell and takes over

cellular metabolism. This forces it to produce new viruses which later on destroys the cell.

Lymphocystis is transmitted via the contents of the burst cells. The fish does not reveal any

strange behavior. Treatment is more successful when the virus is recognized early. The fish

which seem healthy must be observed 60 days in the protected environment.

Abdominal Dropsy: Infectious abdominal dropsy have been extensively studied in

carp. Viruses always infect the fish, but bacteria are always involved, and are seen as the

primary cause. Almost all species of fish can be affected including tilapia species. The

bacteria can survive without a host in water or mud for months. Because they belong to the

normal bacterial flora of the pond, healthy fish can resist them. The fish are in danger only

when starvation, improper diet, cold, or transportation stresses them or if the pond contains

waste products and turbidity. Once the fish is affected, it releases large numbers of bacterias.

Then all other species in the pond are attacked. The belly of the fish is as if it is bloated to the point of bursting. Skin lesions appear as small vesicles along the lateral line, the fish often rock back and forth just under the surface of the water, the ocular reflex is also weaker. The anus is inflamed and puffed out. Fins clamp together. If the kidney reaches the advanced stage then anemia causes the gills to become pale.

Abdominal dropsy of pond fish does not have symptoms. Some of the symptoms described above can appear at once or separately. It is also possible that fish can become emaciated or die without signs. Any bacteria found belong to just a few genera. Usually Gram-negative rods of 1 to 3 microns are found in the fluid from the body cavity, in the liver, spleen, and kidney (Untergasser, 1990).

Furunculosis: This is a septicaemic bacterial disease. It is worldwide, although it occurs mainly among the salmonids. It affects many species of cold water and warm water fishes. This word *furunculosis* comes from the *furunculus* or blisters that occur on the skin of the infected fish. *Furunculus* can also occur in other types of infections. It is also obvious that in case of acute *furunculosis*, furunculus may not be present (Pillay, 1993). *Aeromonas salmonicida*, the causative agent, may survive for days in water. But if there is no carrier fish in the same body of water the bacterial disease will not persist. Positive diagnosis is based on isolation of and identification of causative agent. The agent is certainly a gram-negative non motile rod that ferments selected carbohydrates, produces *cytochrome oxidase* and yields a water-soluble brown pigment of an agar. The incubation period is about 2-4 days, but in chronic cases the period may be extended for several weeks at lower temperatures (Pillay, 1993). This bacterial disease can attack any fish species anywhere in the world. In Africa it

Flexibacter Columnaris Disease.

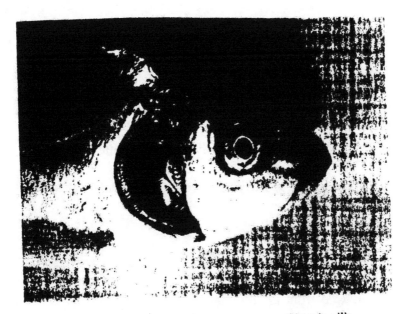

Common Carp affected by Spring Viremia, with pale gills.

can attack the tilapia species, *T. zillii, T. rendallii* from Kenya, *procambrus spp. O. leucostictus* in Uganda, *O. niloticus* any other species that are cultured in Africa. This disease has been found in Asia in countries such as China, Philippines, Thailand and Malaysia.

Columnaris Disease: *Columnaris* disease occurs in acute or chronic form in both cold water and warm water fishes worldwide, and is caused by a bacteria *Flexibacter columnaris*. The highly virulent form attacks the gill tissue and the less virulent ones are mainly responsible for cutaneous infections (Pillay, 1993). The signs of the disease is the discoloration of grey patches in the dorsal fin area. The injury is mainly in the mouth and the head which sometimes become yellow and the injury causes a *gill rot*. The less virulent strains may not show any external signs. This disease can be found in most species of fish everywhere in the world. In Africa it can be found in *tilapia species, O. niger* from Kenya, *procambrus* in Uganda, and many other species that are cultured in Africa and Asia (Kigeya, 1995).

Bacterial Gill Disease: This gill disease is caused by *mycobacteria* and affects Salmonids and fed on dry concentration of powder feed. It is basically caused by bad hygiene in the breeding environment. If the pond has too many food wastes, too high density, and insufficient oxygen, will contribute to survival of the disease.

Usually the diseased fish stops feeding, remains motionless near the surface, the gills are usually smaller and rather dark red in color. The gill filaments secretes a lot of mucous and the opercula is open. In treating this disease, the pond environment should be kept clean, and water should be renewed from time to time. The fish should be given sufficient baths in sulphate at a rate of one gallon to 10 litres of water (Huet, 1986). The acute epidemic may

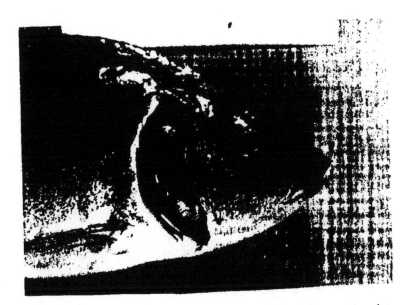

Flexibacter Columnaris Disease- Transmitted from brood fish to off-spring through eggs or sperm.

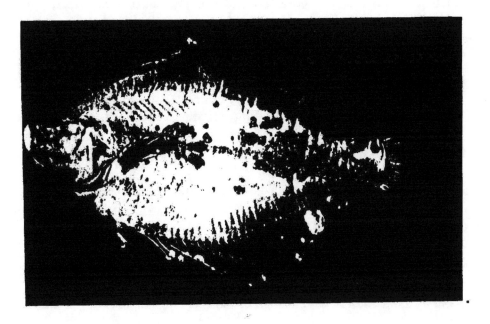

Lymphocystis Nodules. It is a viral disease in several species of fresh water, brackish water, and other marine species of fish. It looks as whitish nodules on fins. This disease is incurable, but prophylaxis can control it.

result into high mortality of up to 50 percent in a single day, *necrosis* of the gill tissue seldom takes place. The recommended diagnostic procedure is the detection of large numbers of *filamentous bacteria* on the gills under a microscope.

The application of adequate clean fish farming environment, avoidance of the overcrowding of the ponds, the re-use of water, maintenance of clean water in ponds will definitely help to reduce the disease in ponds.

Diseases of Fungus Nature

Seprolegnia infection is caused by fungi of genera *Saprolegnia* and *Achlya*, which developed in injured fish, weakened, diseased, or dead fish. This disease can also develop in dead eggs in incubation materials. These fungi can be present in freshwater, but more likely in water containing organic substances. All parasitic fungi live as *saprophytes* on the remains of food and dead fish. *Saprolegnia* affects all species of fish everywhere in the world and all times. All external injuries attract parasitic fungi (Huet, 1986). This disease affects the skin and gills of the cultured fish. There are three major species of *saprolegnia* which are related to the disease: *S. ferax, S. parastica* and *S. diclina*. They reproduce asexually by means of biflagellate spores.

Environmental stress, overcrowding, poor handling and weakness caused by bacteria viral infections, and temperatures have a big role to play in the survival of this fungal disease. This disease can be found in Africa, Asia, Latin America, North America and Europe. In Africa, the disease can attack all fish species that are cultured such as all species of tilapia: *T. zillii, T. rendalli, T. niloticus, T. galilea, T. esculenta, T. pangami, T. andersonii.* Other species that are likely to attract it are *chipati* in Zambia, *T. malanopleura* in Nigeria, *cyprinus carpio*, everywhere in East Africa and many other parts of Africa. As stated earlier, fungal disease can attack any species anywhere in the world. It is necessary therefore to discuss the treatment and the preventative measures of the disease.

Treatment:

To avoid this disease, care must be taken in regard to injuries, long storage in cement ponds, careless handling of cultured fish, diseases, weaknesses, unhealthy surroundings and bad quality water and high stocking of the water body must be avoided (Huet, 1986).

The treatment of cultured fish by giving them baths of (1) potassium permanganate (1 gm per 100 litres) or 22 gallons of water for 60 to 90 minutes; (2) salt bath (10 gm or 1/3 ounce per litre of water for 20 minutes for young fish, 25 gm (1 oz.) per litre of water for 10 minutes for older fish); (3) copper sulphate bath, 5 gm in 10 litres (2 gal. 2 pt.) of water until fish show signs of weakness. (4) Malachite, green bath (zinc-free) 1 gm of malachite green in 450 ml (3 gall.) of water; 1 to 2 ml of solution of malachite solution per litre for 1 hour (Huet, 1986; Pillay, 1993). Malachite green can also be used for treating small ponds, 1 gm of malachite green for 5 to 10 m^3 (6 1/2 to 13 yd^3) of water in *trout*, a lower concentration is used.

The treatment of eggs in incubator is possible to prevent the growth of fungal disease to the incubating eggs by administering daily (5) formalin bath for 15 minutes, 1 to 2 ml of 30 percent formyl should be added (Huet, 1986). Copper oxalate of malachite green can be used to treat fungi when they appear and develop on incubating eggs. In case of treating of the eggs as cited above, the water supply should be cut off. The treatment can also be conducted without touching normal water supply (Huet, 1986; Pillay, 1993).

Gill Rot: This disease is also known as *branchiomycosis*. Fungi of branchyomyces cause the gills to rot, in most *cyprinids* and in *pike*. This disease appears in hot summers in mainly densely stocked ponds which contain abundant organic matter and phytoplankton. At the beginning fish have dark reddish gills, eventually the gills get completely destroyed. In warm weather the development of this fungal disease is extremely rapid.

In treating the stocked fish, one should avoid too densely stocked ponds when the weather is very hot. When the weather is hot, it is advisable to reduce artificial feeding, provide plenty of freshwater. Quicklime should be spread on the pond floor. At least 200 kg or 440 lb. of lime should be used per hectare. The pH should not exceed more than 9.0. It is also possible to use an algicide, such as copper sulphate or benzalkonium chloride. A copper sulphate bath: 1 gm in 10 litres or 2 gallon 1 1/2 pint of water for 10 to 30 minutes. This may eliminate the parasites (Huet, 1986).

Protozoan Caused Diseases

Costiasis: This is a disease which can attack all species of fish from the earliest age. It is very dangerous among young *carp*. This disease develops when fish are densely stocked in a pond, tank and dams. This disease is common in wintering ponds and also in environments where living conditions are unfavorable due to lack of food or too much acid in water. In Salmonid ponds the disease spreads very rapidly during summer, and within a very short time the disease spreads fast and becomes intense.

The affected fish will be covered with a light gray-blue film and red patches show at the affected parts. The gills turn brown and partially destroyed. The fish reduce their eating and their strength is reduced. The weakest fry and fingerlings finally die.

In treating this fish, baths must be given and infected fish is placed in a pond with plenty of food. The fish should not be overstocked. Formalin bath is suggested and some *trout fry* withstand them; 20 to 25 ml (1.2 to 1.5 in^3) of formalin in 100 litres of water for a period of 30 to 45 minutes or 40 ml (2.4 in^3) of formalin in 100 litres of water for 15 minutes (Huet, 1986). It is possible to give salt bath to *trout fry* 10 gm of salt per litre of water for 20 minutes. Doses can be doubled for large fish and baths can take from 10 to 15 minutes.

Whirling Disease: This disease can also be called *Myxosporidiasis*. This type of disease is encouraged by the type of culture. The disease is less rampant in extensive types of *carp farms* in comparison to intensive systems like cages. Intensively stocked polyculture carp ponds in China contain lots of organic manure and *bacterial, fungal,* and *viral diseases* are very common in these (Pillay, 1993).

This disease is mainly in North America, Europe, and attacks *Salmonids*. This disease is dangerous to fish culture as it can lead to high mortality rate in *rainbow trout* and *brook trout* fingerlings. *Brown trout* fingerlings are more resistant to this disease. The causative agent is a *protozoan myxosoma cerebralis*. The spores are found in the mud on the pond bottom where they are more resistant to this disease. The disease cannot be transmitted by eggs, but it is noticed in a pond after fish are stocked in the pond. In contaminated water, small *fry trout* are affected within three days from the time of hatching. When the disease is in the intestines of the young fish, spore release *sporozoites* which are carried by blood to the

cartilage of the head (Huet, 1986).

Signs of the affected fish is that *fingerling trouts* whirl round and round in the same

direction several times and then fall to the bottom of the pond. They come up again and

whirl round and round and sometimes swim normally and then fall to the bottom again. This

goes on for weeks and some fish develop *black tails* caused by the infection. Some

malformation are also noticed in the infected fish, like the *deformation of the spine,*

shortening of the jaws and *the gill cover, bumps,* and *small cavities in the head.*

Steps must be taken to avoid infection as contaminated fish cannot be cured. Once the

farm is infected, it is impossible to rid it of the disease (Huet, 1986). It is recommended to

empty the ponds in September before the spores form in the bodies of the young fish. At this

time the infection is not severe yet. It is also possible to reduce the loss percentage

considerably if one rears fingerlings in large ponds and avoid feeding cultured fish with

artificial feeds.

On the intensive *salmonid farm* only complete disinfection can help to eliminate the

disease. All incubation shed, installations, the storage ponds and tanks and all other materials

used are to be disinfected with quicklime, or calcium cyanamide. According to Huet (1986),

he recommends the use of .5 to 1 kg of calcium cyanamide per square metre, or 5 to 10 tons

per hectare on the bottom. Another way to avoid infection on the farm is to feed the

incubation shed with spring water which in practice can always be protected from

contamination. The fry are fed 6 to 8 weeks in troughs supplied by the same water. The rearing of fingerling trouts in long cement basins which can easily be disinfected is the best way to fight this dreaded whirling disease.

Ichthyophthiriasis: White spot is the most prevalent fish disease. It appears as white spots on fish. Sometime these spots appear as grayish in color. They have a diameter of 0.5-1 mm on the fins and the skin of the fish. Each spot is a bladder containing parasites. These parasites are unicellular organisms called *ichthyophthirius multifiliis*. The parasites penetrate the outer layer (*epidermis*) of the skin. When the parasites move in the skin, irritation is felt in the skin (Duijn, 1973).

The young parasites reproduce themselves by a simple division shortly after penetrating the skin. These parasites feed on red-blood corpuscles extracted from the superficial blood capillaries. When these parasites leave their host they sink to the bottom of the water. They secrete a jelly-like covering about themselves. The reproduction process of these parasites depend on temperature. Where the temperatures are high the reproduction will be very fast. The parasites keep leaving the animals and then attacking them from time to time, increasing the number of the parasites.

Small white specks are noticed on the skin. When the parasite is more serious, the spots become white spots, and the gills can be attacked. The fish jump in the water and try to rid themselves of the parasites by rubbing themselves against the bottom of the pond or against any submerged object (Huet, 1986; Duijn, 1973). A severe attack causes heavy losses among *carp, trout, tilapia,* and other young fish.

The treatment of these parasites are very difficult once these parasites are under the epidermis. Sometimes these can be treated by placing affected fish in a storage tank for many days. According to Duijn (1973), he states that if ponds are many, the affected fish can be changed from one pond to another every 2 to 4 days.

Worm Caused Diseases

Fish Leeches: The blood sucking leech, or *pissicola geometra*, is an external parasite found in calm water. It attacks all species of fish in water. This is a cylindrical worm of 2 or 3 cm in length. According to Huet (1986), it has a sucker at each end of its round body. It attaches itself on the host and keeps on sucking it. When it is filled, it detaches itself from the fish and swims freely in the water. When it is attached to the fish it moves like a caterpillar.

The signs are that the fish will be covered by parasites all over. The fish is weakened through loss of blood. Other *fungi* affect it even more as it is already weak. When parasites are too many, the damage will be very great. The treatment for this type of disease is that if the parasites are many the pond should be emptied and fish bathed. The fish should be put in lysol solutions. Fish must then be rinsed in fresh water. Salt bath can also be given, 10 gm of kitchen salt for 1 litre of water for 20 minutes. Lime bath is the simplest method for a large number of fish in a pond. For a period of 5 seconds, fish are plunged in the water containing 2 gm of quicklime per litre of water. In case the pond dries up, the bottom should be treated with quicklime to kill eggs and leeches still living there.

Ligulosis: This disease is caused by long ribbon-like tape worms. *Ligula intestinalis* is about 15 to 20 cm. It can grow up to 2 feet and 5 inches. It is about 0.6 to 1.5 cm wide.

The disease is met much more in open waters than in fish culture ponds. It attacks numerous species of fish, mainly cyprinids. The disease can be eliminated by preventing water fowl.

Gill fluke-caused disease: The gill flukes, or *dactylogyrus*, is a small flat trematode worm. This worm attacks gills of all types of fish and mainly in ponds, e.g. *carps*. This worm is dangerous to young *carps*. This happens mainly in summer when this worm is found in ponds. This worm makes the gills to swell and turns gray at the edges.

The spawning ponds should only be put under water during spawning periods only. Fish suffering from *Dactylogyrus* can be treated by baths: salt baths at a ratio of 25 gm to 1 oz. per litre of water for about 10 minutes for large fish and 15 gm per litre during 20 minutes for fry. Formalin baths of 0.25 to 0.50 ml per litre of water for 30 minutes for fry and 1 ml per litre of water over 15 minutes for large fish (Huet, 1986).

Fish ponds can be treated with trichlorfon to control blood sucking leeches. Fish ponds also can be treated with trichlorfon, 0.5 g to every m^3 for carp, tench, and eels or 0.2 grams to every m^3 for *trout* and *pike*.

Crustaceans

Argulus or fish lice are parasites for fish. *Argulus* is a small, flat crustacean, green yellow in color and can be up to 8 mm in length. *Argulus foliaceous* is 8 mm long, *Argulus coregoni* is 12 mm in length. These parasites attach themselves to the skin of the fish at the base of the fin by means of hooks and two suckers under the eyes (Huet, 1986).

The sting can cause wounds which open the way for other infections. The harm done by these parasites depends on how many they are on the fish. If the attack is minor then the harm will be very little, but in case of a major attack, these parasites will inflict severe damage and suck a lot of blood which will result in *anemia* which in the end can cause death.

The sting of these parasites will cause red blotches on the skin and the fish will show signs of nervousness and will scratch themselves to get rid of these parasites. Another method of eradicating these parasites is by using *lysol baths*, 1 gm of lysol to 1 litre of water for 40 seconds. The drying of the ponds and then by liming them with quicklime is a good preventive method. In some countries such as Israel, *lindane baths* are given to *carp* during transportation. For a journey which would take 2 to 3 hours, 0.3 gm of *lindane* per cubic metre of water is put in tanks. The fish are tightly loaded (1 kg of carp for 1.5 litres of water, or 2 1/4 lb. of carp for 3 1/4 pt.) and the water should be well aerated. *Lindane* can also be used in ponds without any danger for the carp. The concentration should be 0.015 gm of lindane per one cubic metre of water.

Environmental Diseases

If the water's pH falls below 5.5 the water can little by little become toxic for most of the fish in the pond. From a pH equal to 5.0 mortality in many fish will start. The skin of fish will be covered with a whitish film and will secrete a lot of mucous. The edges of the gills will turn brownish. Certain fish will swim slowly while others will die close to the banks and in a normal position (Huet, 1986).

The pH of such ponds with this danger must be monitored frequently. If pH falls below 5.5 then 500 kg of calcium carbonate must be spread per hectare. Water from melting snow or run-off should not be allowed to enter the pond, mainly if they are surrounded by conifer woods. If pH is above 9.0 should be considered dangerous for the fish. This can be caused by pollution and also in concrete tanks, if the concrete tank is too fresh. It can also occur as a result of distribution of quicklime. The assimilation of the abundant submerged vegetation in the bright tropical sunshine can also cause the *alkalinity*. It can be corrected, however, by controlling the amount of vegetation in the water. This will reduce the *alkalinity* in the water.

Temperature causes great damage in lakes and seas where high temperatures are experienced. At times this is exaggerated as fish in some locations can withstand temperatures between 10 to 12°C (Huet, 1986). It is important also to be careful with water whose temperatures are below 10°C. This will lead to disruptions of varieties of metabolic conditions, such as anoxia, fright, forced exertion, anaesthesia, temperature changes and injury.

Temperatures above or below the limits, as stated earlier, result into stress to animals in the water. Dissolved gases, including oxygen, generally decrease insolubility of toxic compounds. But on the other hand, increased solubility will follow the rising temperatures. The minimum water quality necessary to maintain fish are: (Pillay, 1993)

pH range	6.7 - 8.6 (extremes 6.0 - 9.0)
Free total CO_2	3 ppm or less
Ammonia	0.02 ppm or less
Alkalinity	at least 20 ppm (as $CaCO_3$)

There are differences in tolerance limits of different species. Levels of tolerance of other elements are chlorine 0.003 ppm, hydrogen sulphide: 0.001 ppm, nitrate (NO_2), 100 ppb, in soft water (Pillay, 1993).

Treatment:

Eradication of diseases from a fish culture farm requires a well organized program. Chemical treatment may assist in eradicating diseases and in controlling *heterotrophic pathogens* of animals under stress. This type of treatment will have adverse effects on biological filters in some recirculating systems which may adversely affect *algae* in the culture systems. Some advanced countries such as U.S.A. restrict the use of chemical in treating fish which is to be used for food. Some of these countries approve only the use of *salt, acetic,* and *sulfamerazine* on food fish.

The chemical characteristic of water will affect the chemotherapeutic treatment and this must be assessed before chemical treatment is applied. Before using chemical treatment, it must be tested on a small number of animals to see how resistant they could be to such treatment.

The continuous feeding of fish with food in which antibiotics are included is discouraged. These antibiotics may be served only when needed and for only at the prescribed treatment levels and for a limited period.

Commercial medications are more recommended if available. They are easy to use and less expensive. Medicated feeds can be made on the farm. These can be made by suspending the drug in oil such as cod liver oil and then coating the daily ration of feed pellets with the mixture of oil and drugs. The use of disease control in aquaculture, bath and dip treatments are much more applicable and common.

The fish should be dipped for short duration varying from a few seconds to about 5 minutes, are recommended for diseases such as *brood stocks*. After dipping the animals should be rinsed in clean water. They should then be released in free clean water.

Sanitation:

Sanitary conditions in an aquaculture farm is of vital importance in preventing the outbreak of diseases. Monitoring the cleanliness of the pond water is extremely important. There are three acceptable methods of disinfection: (i) *ozonation*, (ii) *ultraviolet irradiation*, and (iii) *chlorination*. When the farm has been affected by an infectious disease, then disinfecting the farm and keeping it clean all the time is very important.

The main reason for maintaining these sanitary conditions is the fact that disease will be prevented from spreading to others. Eggs can be disinfected to prevent the spread of diseases to other locations. The sanitary condition prevents the spread of infectious diseases by preventing the transmission of pathens from parents to any other stock which is not yet attacked. This might involve retaining newly imported stock from outside. When such infectious diseases are detected and suspected to have been introduced in the farm by imported stock animals, then keeping them in confinement for sometime is warranted. This method of prevention is used more in research than in commercial farming. The confinement facilities must be located distances away from the commercial farm. This will keep the suspected disease away from the farm. All equipment, materials, or individuals from the confinement facilities must be completely disinfected.

Chlorination at 200 mg per litre for two hours is recommended. Lower concentration is more effective if the fish are dipped longer than two hours. These methods are utilized in small volumes of water rather than ponds or lakes.

Immunization:

Vaccines sometimes are used to immunize fish to prevent the diseases from spreading. *Licensed vaccines* are available in many locations and are utilized very frequently to prevent the disease infections. Such methods can only be used by technically qualified experts. They must diagnose the disease precisely and determine the cure. The amount of the *vaccines* must be measured precisely. If the amount is too much could destroy the animals in the water. As stated before the amount should be tried on a small number of animals to detect the resistance.

It should be remembered that *immunization* of fish is done by a variety of methods, but *immunization by immersion* of fish is more common, successful, and cost effective. There are other methods such as *spray-shower vaccination, injection vaccination* are some of the methods that can be used. The *immune* response takes two to four weeks, under normal conditions, for protective immunity to develop after the introduction of antigenic stimulation is done. The fish that have been vaccinated can retain this immunity for well over 300 days. But if temperatures are high it will encourage the antibody production.

Genetic Resistance to Disease:

In Africa, and in many Third World nations where there is a mixture of different variety of animals is helpful in developing strains of fish that can be resistant to certain infections. In most big rivers and lakes in Africa, Asia and South and Central America, there is a considerable amount of mixing of strains of fish. This mixing of fish is quite beneficial in developing types of fish that are resistant to infection. The types of resistance to disease of certain fish in ponds, rivers, dams and lakes can be measured experimentally.

Some of these strains develop other bacterial gill infections despite the fact that they may have acquired resistance to some diseases, such as *furunculosis*. Fish such as *stealhead trout* are resistant to bacterial kidney disease, but they are most susceptible to '*vibrio anquillarum*' (Pillay, 1993). The idea of avoiding diversity of fish in the selection process leads to the loss of fish resistance to disease. When fish survive after resisting a certain disease it will have high trait value. But some of these strains of fish may remain as disease carriers. This is detrimental to other animals that are not resistant to this particular disease.

In lakes such as Wamala, Kyoga, Albert and Victoria, run-offs have from time to time deposited a great deal of domestic wastes such as animal droppings, human excrements, industrial wastes and human bodies that are left lying all over the countryside, whenever fighting takes place. During Tanzania-Uganda war of 1979, 1986 and Ruanda war in 1994, 1995, many human corpses were seen floating on these lakes. Such types of deposition wastes are bound to introduce disease in these water bodies. Due to lack of technological sophistication, and research no study or studies might have been conducted by scientists to discover the type of diseases these strains of fish carry. It is also possible that due to diversification of fish varieties in these lakes and rivers, that such diseases could have been resisted.

In many instances in the countryside, most homes in Africa, Asia and Latin America have their toilets situated outside the main residential houses. These toilets are located on higher grounds and when the underground water from these toilets percolates through the ground, drains in rivers, ponds, dams and even lakes that are situated in valleys below. Diseases are bound to be carried by these underground drainage systems to water bodies in valleys. Studies should be conducted to discover the types of water in our rivers, ponds, dams and lakes, and how this water affects the fish that inhabit such locations.

Farm Disinfection:

When a disease is detected on an aquaculture farm, the farmer destroys the whole stock and disinfects the whole pond. This has to be done before re-stocking the farm again. This type of disinfecting the fish facility would be improbable if reinfection is possible from the nearby open waters and if the economic cost of loss due to the disease is less than the cost of disinfection.

It is easier to disinfect small hatcheries, tank farms, dams, ponds, and raceways, but large lake-like ponds and dams may be difficult to disinfect, due to the amount of water and the likelihood of re-infection from various sources. It is all the more difficult for such method of disinfection to be used in Africa and in many Third World nations such as India, Malaysia, Philippines, Thailand and many others. In these nations water bodies below in the valleys get contaminated from various sources. Some sources could be agricultural disinfectants, fertilizers, chemicals, or domestic wastes. In many Asiatic nations, agricultural fertilizers have been a great source of water contamination. In countries such as China, Taiwan, Korea, Singapore, Philippines, fertilizers are used very extensively and have contaminated water bodies including fish ponds. The unfortunate part is that their technology is not yet sophisticated to be able to clean these water bodies.

In Africa, on the other hand, agricultural fertilizers and chemicals have not contaminated water bodies as much as they have done in Asia. This is so because many African farmers have not started using fertilizers, and other chemicals in their agriculture. But in a few nations such as Egypt, Liberia, South Africa, Nigeria, Uganda, Kenya, Tanzania, and Zimbabwe, many farmers have started using these fertilizers. At this juncture water bodies in Africa do not show too much chemical contamination, but it is soon coming up to the level of many Third World nations. Africa's major source of water contamination is from domestic wastes, animal droppings, human excrements underground drainage which spring from toilets, industrial wastes such as oil, tars and other materials that come from industries. These are the great sources of contamination in Africa.

In disinfecting large ponds slaked lime at the rate of 2 tons per hectare of wet pond bottom should be applied. Several treatments may be needed to disinfect earthen ponds, dams and tank farms because some chemicals may not be effective in mud. For some *bacterias, viruses,* and non-specific *protozoa* in ponds, Finlay (1978) recommended 1 percent *sodium hydroxide* and 0.1 percent teepol. The detergent encourages the penetration of the disinfectant through the soil. A high pH of about 11 or more is necessary for such disinfectant to function. The following disinfectants can be used in ponds, tanks, dams and large lake-like ponds.

Disinfectant	Application	Working Strength	Effective Against
Chlorine	Concrete, fiberglass, butyl-lined ponds, nets, footbaths.	1% - 2%	Bacteria, fungi, viruses
Sodium hydroxide	Earthen ponds, concrete, fiberglass, butyl-lined ponds, nets, foot baths.	1% with 0.1% teepol 0.5 gallon/m^2 (2.28 l/m^2)	Bacteria, viruses, protozoa
Iodophors	Concrete, fiberglass, butyl-lined ponds, nets, angling, equipment.	250 ppm	Bacteria, viruses
Quartermary ammonium compounds Hyamine, Roccal, etc.	Clothing, hands ova nuts, clothing, hands	100 ppm manufacturer's instructions	Bacteria
Calcium oxide	Earthen ponds, fiberglass, concrete, butyl-lined ponds	As powder: 380 g/m^2	Protozoa (Whirling disease)

Based on (Hnath, 1983).

CHAPTER VIII

INTEGRATION OF AQUACULTURE WITH

CROP AND ANIMAL FARMING

Fish farming originated in China about 2500 years before Christ. Chinese were peasant farmers, but as Chinese migrated to different parts of Asia, they transported this system of farming in other Asiatic nations such as Philippines, Thailand, Korea, Singapore, India and in many other countries.

Fish farming in Asia has always been conducted on a part-time basis. Farm ponds, dams and reservoirs were constructed as sources of water where fish farming could be grown. Fish were grown in channels, rice farms, in dams and in many farm ponds. Many countries noticed that it would be very economical to integrate fish with rice in their rice fields.

The labor that was required to take care of the rice fields was enough for both rice and fish, without any extra labor. Farm fish feeds that would drop to the bottom was used to fertilize the rice fields. Because this integrated fish farming provides more employment, nutrition and income of rural population in Asia and Africa, it is important to examine it very closely.

Integrated fish farming is being practiced in some African countries such as Malagasy Republic, where rice is grown and used as the staple food. Central African Republic and Zambia are some of the other countries which practice integrated fish farming.

In Malagasy Republic, integrated farming has been going on for over 80 years. They rear fish by mixing up different types of fish such as *carp, crucian carp, tilapia* like *T. mossambica*, and production is based on the raising of fry. The stocking is light and reaches probably 150 to 250 fish per hectare (Huet, 1986). Manuring and artificial feeding are not used much, but when they are utilized the production reaches about 200 to 250 fish per hectare.

Integrated fish farming, as stated earlier, has not been adopted by many African nations. There are a few nations in Africa which practice it, such as Zambia, Zaire, and Malawi. In Zambia, the aim was to keep the weeds down by using *T. melanopleura* and in Zaire, Katanga province, integrated fish farming is being practiced extensively. Species such as *T. macrochir, T. melanopleura*, and *Haplachromis mellandi* are produced in Katanga province.

The Importance of Integrated Fish Farming and Animals in Africa

Although integrated fish farming has been introduced to Africa by countries discussed earlier on, this type of aquaculture is still limited to only very few locations on the continents. In countries where integrated fish farming has been introduced, it is doing very well. If each of the African countries give priority to fish farming, probably integrated fish farming would be making vast differences in many rural people's lives.

This idea of integrated fish farming originated in Asia. It started in China, because China had a great number of pigs which supplied necessary droppings which were used as fertilizers for both rice and fish. From China, it spread to other countries in Asia such as Philippines, Thailand, Singapore, India and Indonesia.

All materials that were required for integrated fish farming in Asia are available in Africa.

This involves (i) vegetable gardening using aquatic vegetables such as water spinach or water chestnut in ponds, (ii) land vegetables can be grown on the banks of the ponds. This will be easy for the aquaculturist to feed the fish in the ponds. (iii) Sugar cane can be grown in between the ponds. This will be easy for fish in ponds to get their food. Sugar cane will provide shade for the fish in ponds. Although sugar cane can be useful they can also breed predators like snakes and other animals that can eat fish from ponds. Animals like otters, eagles, frogs that will move easily from sugar cane plantation to the ponds can be very dangerous to fish. In Africa where they have heavy rains almost everyday, sugar cane bushes will be so thick that they might be more harmful than useful. (iv) Mulberry trees that can be used to raise silkworms which can be utilized as fertilizers for crops, but leaves can also be used as feeds for fish in ponds. Such trees are common in sub-saharan Africa. Such trees will prove to be useful for integrated fish farming.

In Africa we have trees that can be very useful for fish. Mulberry trees are common in Uganda, Kenya, East of Lake Victoria and because these surroundings are good in terms of trees, they can promote integrated fish farming in Africa. The leaves of these trees are good as feeds to silkworms, which serve as fertilizers and feeds to fish.

There are abundant productions of fruit trees such as bananas, papayas, and coconuts which are grown between ponds, such trees are common everywhere in Africa. Uganda,

Kenya, Tanzania, Zaire, Nigeria, Cameroon have plenty of such fruit trees. These trees can act as feeds for fish and in return the fish pond water can be used to irrigate these plantations.

Integration with chicken and pig farming can be encouraging to integrated fish farming in Africa. Almost every country of Africa like Egypt, Sudan, Mali, Morocco, Uganda, Kenya, Tanzania, Zambia, Ghana, Nigeria, Angola, Zimbabwe, South Africa, chicken and pigs are readily found. If integrated fish farming could be practiced along with these animal farming, fish production will be promoted. Droppings of such animals will be utilized as fertilizers and feeds for fish.

Aquatic weeds that are taken from these ponds can be used as feeds to these chicken and pigs. Integration of fish production with ducks are equally important in promoting fish production in Africa.

Integrated Farming of Fish and Animals

Although fish farming is integrated with the growing of domesticated animals, but pigs and duck raisings have been most successful. In China and many other Asiatic nations, pig production is of great significance in integrated fish farming. Pigs are considered as costless fertilizers in China. They form the most important source of domestic manure. Farmers in Africa, as stated earlier, will never have any problem in conducting integrated fish farming because pigs are readily available. For individuals who want to practice fish farming have to start raising domestic pigs and ducks.

Cattle and chicken are also very important. These animals provide the necessary wastes to promote the production of integrated fish farming. Ducks love living and playing in water. Thus ducks choose to utilize and spend most of their time playing, swimming and eating from the ponds. Ducks fertilize the ponds with their excrement.

In all the countries of Africa where integrated fish farming is done, most well established fish farms use herbivorous or omnivorous species. The common species used are Chinese carps, the *Catfish Pangastius, Indian carps* and *tilapia species*.

The benefits of integrated fish farming are (i) the easy access to the manure which fertilizes the pond and produces plankton which feeds the fish. The domestic animals in Africa make integrated fish farming easy, because (ii) fish eating is made easy due to the availability of domesticated animals which provide the droppings for feeds. (iii) Fruit trees, vegetables and other crops are available close to the banks of ponds.

Crops such as groundnuts, corn, sugar cane, bananas, and mulberry trees are planted close to the banks and these act as feeds for fish in Africa. Ponds are fairly crowded as tilapia species are prolific producers. It is ironic that the major constraint hindering the rapid development of *tilapia culture* is the shortage of high quality seed for restocking. This is a great problem in Africa today than it has been before, as many African farmers are becoming interested in fish farming. Because many people have desired fish fry for stocking in their fish farms, the fry are becoming too few for the people. In many African countries, particularly in Uganda, the government is selecting a few farmers and train them to produce fry. These farmers will be responsible to sell fry to their fellow farmers (Kigeya, 1995).

Fry production is a booming business in the Eastern countries and fry are sold in markets everywhere in East Asia. But in Africa, because fish farming is fairly new to the people, the governments try to encourage farmers by providing them with free fry from government fish ponds. It has reached to a point now when the government cannot meet the demand for fry. The government started selling the fry to farmers so as to meet the cost of producing them.

Another alternative is the one stated earlier that certain farmers are selected to grow fry. In growing these fish fry, integrated fish farming would be very profitable. Animals would be reared along with fry production. The animals will produce their droppings which will act as fertilizers to the fish ponds. But plants such as cassava, sweat potatoes, yams, sugar cane, and other plants will be grown close to the banks of the ponds. This will make it easy for fish farmers to produce fry, as there will be plenty of feed supply.

This system will not only increase the farmers who participate in fish farming, but it will also increase income of the farmers involved in fish fry production. Usually fish farmers specialize in fry production or adult fish production. Some people, particularly those whose income is good, can do both the production of fry and also the production of fish.

Farmers who practice this type of farming must understand that fry cannot be mixed with regular fish production and let them grow together. The two types must be located in separate ponds. This will help farmers to keep fry of the same type in one pond. Farmer buyers usually come asking for tilapia fry and that kind of fish must be produced. If farmers mix many types of fry, it will be difficult to separate them at harvesting time. If fish fry production is made permanent in the country it will encourage those who want to grow fish fry, and make it a full-time occupation.

In recent years the major advances in tilapia production have occurred where the fry and fingerling production have been separated from the growing and fattening stages (McAndrew, 1983). This enabled many new methods of production to be brought into play.

Earthen Ponds:

Fry production in earthen ponds is the widely used method in the world. The poorest method is the one in which production is found in undrainable ponds in which there is no routine cropping system (McAndrew, 1983). Good and successful method is the one where production is done in drainable brood ponds.

There is another method of production in net enclosures which is also known as Hapas. This method is in use in Philippines. This system uses fine nylon net enclosures which are also called hapas or mosquito netting. While in this confinement, the fish are fed with rice bran, chicken feed, and some other vegetable feeds. Integrated fish farming techniques could also be utilized. Ducks, pigs, chicken and cow droppings could be used. This will enhance fast growing of fry. The more these fry are fed, the faster they will mature and the earlier they will be harvested. The reported yields from these systems are between 200 fry per square metre (Garcia, 1982) and 880 fry/m^2. The stocking density and the sex ratio plays a big part in fry production and appears to be 4-5 per metres. Any further intensification may result in a decrease in fry numbers.

Fry production can also be done in tanks, but the highest levels of production are found in combined tank and Hapa systems, where large tanks are divided into separate net enclosures. This allows accurate stock control as brood stocks are easily managed. The system uses total seed collection methods whereby female broods are released manually, and are transferred to all-female tanks.

Basic Need in Rural Community

Integrated fish farming would be helpful to the African farmers to deal with his environment and socio-economic situation. The basic need in the rural communities in Africa is to deal with inconsistency and uncertainty of the agricultural situation. Agriculture is the backbone of the economy of both the rural and urban communities of Africa. Sometimes farmers in Africa are vulnerable to the business people and many other people around who make a living from the hands of a farmer. Many of these so called business people go to rural communities and buy agricultural products from the farmers at a deplorable low price and resell them in cities or even abroad at higher prices. These farmers are taken advantage of from time to time. It is important to change this situation so that farmers earn what they labor for. It may necessitate farmers working together with other farmers to find other creative ways of dealing with their rural problems.

Usually such changes do not come so easily and certainly not by the outsiders, it requires cultural sensitivity and focus. It requires intensive programs, and very serious, contextualized projects.

Objectives of the Integrated Fish Farming

There are three basic objectives of the integrated fish farming in Africa, namely:

I.   To establish central resource base for integrated farms in the rural communities of Africa. The roles the integrated fish farms are to play in rural Africa are as follows:

1.   These integrated fish farms may provide economic support base for all communities and their development in the whole continent. This will include salaries for all employees on those farms and all those involved in the running of those communities. Costs for extension teachers, and all other overhead costs of operating these community development programs will be paid for.

2.   These farms will be experimental centers for agriculture for these communities, technology and management principles. The goal for the experimentation is to evaluate the feasibility of agricultural methods and technology for use in Africa. The experimentation will also aim at adapting new methods and technology to local rural communities on the continent.

3.   These farms will not only be for experimentation, but will also apply these ideas in other parts of Africa and probably in other parts of the world. Application *forms* will be developed which will be appropriate for Africa. These farms will become centers for applied technology, agriculture, economics, and management theory. The staff employed on these integrated farms will be trained on these farms. These individuals in turn will teach the local residents using the extension methods.

4. These farms will be models for integrated farming as well as complete development for the community and the development projects, at the village levels. Everything done on these farms will focus on the replication at the rural community level in Africa.

5. The farms will provide holistic community development projects at the rural community levels, which will be supported by the communities at the village level. If these farms in various communities do not succeed in one country, they will probably not succeed in other countries on the continent.

6. These farms will act as the marketing systems for the local village communities. These integrated farms in each community will reach further and wider in the marketing of products than any other marketing system in existence in the communities. These farms will provide advice and guidance in marketing as well as becoming new developers of new potential marketing systems for these local communities. The ongoing evaluation of, and the adaptation of the marketing system is important for the future viability of the community development projects that are likely to occur at the village level.

II.   The second major objective is to establish other resource bases for community development at the village level. These other local resource bases are essentially smaller integrated farms which use the central farm or farms as models. The focus of each of these resource bases is to establish a self-supporting resource base at village level which will equip and enable a group of local people to do ongoing community development at the local community level.

The eco-system co-ops are run by volunteers from the village community who both improve their own socio-economic situation by others in the co-ops and work to solve a variety of local community problems, using the resources, finance, knowledge, technology, products--(pigs, fish, ducks and trees etc.), management skills and others, which are acquired by learning how to operate successfully the central community resource centers. The eco-system co-ops deal with the development of a small group of volunteers. When they have progressed enough they then address the various needs of the community using resources at their disposal in their village level.

III.   The third major basic objective of the integrated fish farms is to enable the members of the local community to reach out and do community development, projects in the local village.

These local community projects may be extended to other local villages. The nature of these projects will depend mainly on the needs of the community, and also on the creativity of the community residents.

Methods for Achieving These Objectives

The projects will basically be replicating the major central project. Whatever the central project did, the rural community projects will also do.

The first methodology to be utilized would be to conduct a research of the central project. Whatever the central project did, the stages it went through, the infrastructures of the sites for the new projects, all these should be seriously taken into consideration.

The second stage would be to purchase land in the rural areas where these rural projects are to be established. After buying the land, fish ponds will be dug, pig pens will be built, a tilapia spawning and sex reversal system will be set up, a duck breeding and raising system will be built on the fish ponds, a pig production system (fish or pigs) will be set up.

In Africa, also we have plenty of chicken, pigs, cows and goats, all these have to be integrated in this new project or projects. By the end of the second year, this rural project should be self-sufficient. At this time this project should be in position to support people of the community, in terms of employment, and fish consumption.

In the third year, 10 projects can be planned for, and in the fourth year, 10 more projects will be planned for. It is expected that these projects will take 2-3 years to be fully self-supporting. In the second or third year, this rural project should be in position to establish appropriate community development projects in those local neighborhoods. This type of local projects will become the ongoing community development resource center for this local neighborhood. The central project will become the consulting farm of the surrounding rural areas.

Important Principles to Remember

There are a few basic principles the integrated fish farming employees must consider:

(1) It is important to remember that the real solution to the people of Africa is to get people in these communities to work together for a common good. Thus the emphasis of the major central center is to set up cooperatives of people who will be willing to work together and develop a resource base from which to help the whole community.

(2) The central farm employees and management realize that one thing is needed that for the continuation of initial community development project is capable of acting as a local agent for change in that community.

(3) For the integrated fish farming to succeed, culturally related groups must be willing to work together. People should at least have the same language, staffed by people from the same ethnic groups who completely accept each other without reservation.

(4) It takes time and effort to help people change. Development in the community cannot be successful by getting orders from top to bottom. Orders should not come from government officials down to the rural farmers. Ideas and all decisions should originate from the grassroots to the top. Development that originates from rural farmers themselves will be sustainable.

(5) All employees and the administrators of each of these projects will originate from these communities where these integrated fish farming projects are established. When the administrators and the workers of these projects come from these communities, people will accept these projects as belonging to them. They will do everything to make sure that these projects succeed. Projects that are participatory in nature, culturally sensitive have the potential of local development and sustainability.

(6) It is equally important to understand that integrated fish farming projects based on traditional village setting and whose organization and existence are based on the knowledge and capabilities of the indigenous people, such projects are likely to survive. The people feel that it is their idea and creation, thus they will do everything within their power, to make their project sustainable. It is extremely important that in every project initiated in the community,

the indigenous people must be part of it. Indigenous people should not be merely employees of the project, but should be the owners, the decision makers, the planners and the employers of all other people who join the project from outside the community. Outsiders should also be involved in such projects but merely as advisors, not as the owners. The decisions to hire or to fire individuals should be left in the hands of the indigenous people within that particular community.

Many times people from outside the community or even outside the country will want to make themselves very knowledgeable and look at the local people as ignorant. At times such people try to dominate the indigenous residents in their community. They will always want to be appointed as the managers of these projects, but such people are enemies of these projects, because as soon as they leave the community, the projects will not have able people to run them because they were not groomed for such responsibilities.

This is what the Europeans did in Africa. The whites were managers of companies, projects, principals of schools, superintendents of hospitals, vice-chancellors of universities and local people were just menial employees. When the time came for the Europeans to leave the country, the local people had no necessary experiences. The results were very obvious. Everywhere the Africans took over, many times dictatorship took over, fighting took over the rural neighborhoods. Forests were filled with bodies of people because leaders were not groomed in what they were expected to do when the whites were still in Africa. Whites never wanted to work with blacks. They always wanted to keep them in ignorance. Whites knew that if they worked with blacks, nationals would be as informed as the whites and probably take over. It is unfortunate that this happened and it has haunted the continent to this day.

Thus if integrated fish farming projects are managed by people from outside the community, they will end up in the same form of confusion and probably failure. Although community participation was given lip service early in the 1950's and 60's, in the process of community development efforts, it was accorded significance by the United Nations popular participation program in the 1970's. Two United Nations documents, namely "Popular Participation in Development" published in 1971 and "Popular Participation in Decision Making for Development," were the major publications that advocated the sharing of powers by the indigenous people. These two documents formalized global thinking about community development (Gustafson, 1989).

Hans Munkner has stated that after 30 years of rural development of the rural poor farmers have deteriorated instead of improving (Munkner, 1978). In 1979 FAO report on the participation of the rural poor in the rural development is very small and the poor farmers are not granted opportunities in decision making in matters that affect their development (FAO, 1979).

Integrated fish farming can only be successful by complete participation of the indigenous residents. The community farmers should be the administrators who make decisions for their projects.

The Uses of Ducks in the Integrated Fish Farming

Fish cultivation was brought in Africa from foreign nations, e.g. China, Britain, France and Germany (Huet, 1986). *Trout* has been raised in cold water in Morocco and Kenya since World War I.

Fish farming has been practiced on subsistence level by African farmers in Uganda since 1931, and Zaire in Katanga since 1946 (Huet, 1986). But between 1953 and 1960, the production of fish halted a little in Africa. This was due to the fact that farmers harvested small sized fish from ponds. The smallness of fish in ponds depended on the overpopulation of the African fish ponds where *Tilapia* was raised in crowded ponds. One of the constraints of *Tilapia* production is overpopulation. *Tilapia* are prolific in their production. They multiply very fast and if not controlled, the pond will be crowded in less than six months. This crowding in ponds is a hindrance in fish growth. Usually farmers use other fish such as *Nile perch* to reduce the amount of fish in ponds. *Nile perch* are prolific producers as well. They keep *Tilapia* controlled, but become dominant themselves. This has happened in some parts in Uganda in Lake Victoria. *Nile perch* consume all young *Tilapias* and indeed reduces the number. But because *Nile perch* has large supply of food, they multiply instead and dominate the whole water body. Between 1953 to 1970 fish farming in some parts of Africa declined, due to overpopulation of *Tilapia*. In some parts of the world, fish farming was booming. In Asiatic nations like China, Taiwan, Malaysia, Thailand, Philippines, Hong Kong fish farming was booming because of the introduction of the integrated fish farming system. As stated earlier, integrated fish farming system can only be successful if ducks, pigs, cattle, kirchen, and other animals are readily available on the farm. This integrated fish farming is very scientifically calculated. The more of these animals are available, the more the fish ponds will be fertilized, the more fish production will be promoted. Ducks have been raised on fish ponds in Europe and Asia for centuries. Ducks and fish are compatible. In European nations such as Hungary, Czechoslovakia, Poland and the German Democratic Republic, ducks have been raised and used on fish ponds. The results have always been very good. Fish production increased.

There are two ways of keeping ducks on fish ponds. One is to allow them free access to the whole pond area, the other is to confine them to certain enclosures (Pillay, 1993). When the ducks are allowed freedom to swim freely all around the pond, they will leave their droppings in the pond. This will assist in fertilizing the pond. These droppings are evenly distributed over the whole pond. The ducks also are allowed to forage around the whole pond for food organisms (Pillay, 1993). This could be utilized in Africa.

Small duck houses are built on or near the ponds with facilities to provide ducks with food. This option of keeping these ducks in confinement is preferred by most farmers in Africa. Most of the enclosures will be on water and only a quarter of these are on land. Some of these droppings fall directly into the pond, and the rest is to be washed into it. The circulation of water in the pond distributes the manure and the manured water.

The most common specie used in the duck fish culture are *herbivores* and *omnivores*. Ducks in Taiwan are raised on fish ponds for eggs also. About 2000-4000 ducks are raised per hectare of ponds (Pillay, 1993). Egg lying ducks start laying eggs until they are two years and after which they are sold (Pillay, 1993). The species of fish cultivated in Taiwan are the *Chinese carps, Grass carps, Silver carp* and the *big head*. There are other varieties of fish that are grown in Taiwan and these are *Tilapia nilotica, Tilapia mossambica* and the *grey*

Mullet.

Fish and ducks are at an advantage if they are simultaneously reared.

(1) The duck's droppings on the surface of the ponds provide excellent organic

manure for the water and the bottom of the pond. This results in abundance of plankton and

other food by which the water animals can profit.

(2) The digging the bottom of some sections, the ducks contribute to the reduction of

water vegetation and increases the development of duck weeds (Huet, 1986).

(3) The parts where the ducks dig the mud are stirred up and the nutrients included

therein are released in solution and increase natural productivity in the ponds.

(4) Feeds which are distributed to ducks but are not eaten, fall to the bottom of the

pond and can be eaten by fish like carps, and those which are not consumed become manure.

(5) In tropical regions, the ducks do eliminate *mollusks* in depth of about 40 to 50 cm

and this reduces *bilharzia*. In all these assist in fish farming production (Huet, 1986).

The rearing of ducks on ponds is practiced in parts of Europe, Asia and Africa. In

Africa ducks are reared on ponds in Zambia, Zimbabwe, Malagasy Republic, Morocco and in

few other countries. In some countries of Africa, ducks are just reared but not on ponds.

Such types of ducks could be useful if ponds could be started in those locations.

Sometimes poultry could be as useful as ducks are, in promoting fish production. This

is greatly used in Far Eastern countries where fish farming is practiced among fish farmers.

In Africa, in almost every nation, poultry is practiced. There are more poultry in Africa than

there are ducks. In which case poultry in Africa could be more useful in promoting fish production than ducks can. This has not been tried on the continent in respect to integrated fish farming, but yet it is of great potential.

At present, African fish farmers use chicken droppings as fertilizers. They take these droppings, put them in a bag and tie them on a post in one corner of the pond. They then let this bag hang into the water. The droppings turn into solutions and spread all over the pond. If poultry could be reared on fish ponds just like ducks, they could easily serve the same purpose in respect to integrated fish farming. I am optimistic that using chicken droppings would be more successful than using duck droppings. There are more chickens than ducks in Africa and almost every farmer has chickens in his or her home. If every farmer could put to use all these, fish production will be greatly promoted.

Pigs could also be raised on banks of ponds and will in the same way assist in promoting fish production as ducks do. Pigs have special significance in China. They are considered as costless fertilizer factory. Pigs manure in China represents the main source of homemade fertilizer. Many farmers raise pigs to meet the needs of crop farming, including fish farming. Pigs' houses are located on ponds' banks. In aquatic plants from the ponds, and other water bodies, including crop wastes can be used for feeding the pigs. Part of the pig manure can be used for fertilizing the pond and the rest of it could be used in fertilizing other agricultural fields.

In almost all integrated farms, *herbivorous* or *omnivorous* types of fish are cultivated. The common species are the *Chinese carps, catfish Pangasius, Indian carps* and a few *Tilapia species* are also being used (Pillay, 1993). The embankments of fish ponds will facilitate the pigs' cages and the planting of fruit trees, vegetables, or other crops. In some countries like

China, embankments can be even 10 meters wide, and usually are planted with groundnuts,

vegetables, colza, corn, sugar cane, mulberry trees, bananas, and castor. The slopes are

planted with grass which can be tied to *grass carps* and other animals. Pig sties are located

on the embankments of ponds, but the number of pigs reared differ from location to location.

In China there are about 45-73 pigs per hectare, but some farms have up to 90 pigs per

hectare. Each pig produces 7-8 tons per year (Pillay, 1993).

The usefulness of pigs on the integrated fish farms will usually depend on the feed

stuffs produced from the ponds. There are aquatic plants such as water hyacinths, Opomosa,

pistia, wolffia, Lemna, and Azolla are grown and are usually utilized as feeds for pigs. They

can be mixed with rice bran, bananas, coconut meal, soybean wastes, fish meal,a nd are fed to

pigs.

Integrated Fish Farming and the Rearing of Cattle in Africa

Cows are numerous in Africa and are probably more in number than either ducks or

pigs. Since there are cows everywhere in almost every country on the continent, it is most

likely that they can be more useful in promoting integrated fish farming than what ducks and

pigs can do. Ducks and pigs are being used in Asia because they are many and can supply

adequate manure as opposed the cow's manure.

In most countries of Africa like Uganda, Kenya, Tanzania, Zaire or the Democratic

Republic of Congo, Nigeria, Ghana, Malawi, Zimbabwe, South Africa and many other

countries, have cows roaming everywhere in the rural areas. In places like Karamoja in

Uganda, Turkana in Kenya, Masailand in Kenya and Tanzania, Sukumaland in Tanzania, cows are quite innumerable. They are, therefore, a potential for promoting integrated fish farming. In Asiatic countries people use ducks, pigs, for providing manure to fertilize fish ponds; in Africa, however, cows, chickens, pigs and ducks are available which can make integrated fish farming possible.

Since time immemorial, cows-keepers in Africa had no regard for seafoods. Many of these people lived on milk and meat. They regarded other people who made a living from other occupations as poor people. They disrespected them, and had nothing to do with them. The herders, as the cow-keepers were called, regarded themselves as royal, kings, princes and princesses and all other people who were outside this group were servants. The fishermen were, among all people, the most despised. The herders regarded fish eating as low, and unacceptable in their circles, because it was food for lowly and poor individuals (Kigeya, 1995). This historical background of herders still persists today.

In Africa, herders do not care about fish eating, leave along fish ponds. Fish ponds were established in most parts of Uganda, but there were few fish ponds in Ankole, in Karamoja, in Turkana, Rwanda, in Sukumaland and in Masainland where cow rearing preoccupied the minds of the herders. Because herders were not accustomed to eating fish, they did not care about digging fish ponds even when they became popular elsewhere in Africa (Kigeya, 1995).

Africans are generally fish eaters, but there are a few people on the continent who still regard fish eating as unacceptable. They feel fish smells too much. Although it is true that some fish stink too much, but it is not that which prevent herders from eating it. Twenty-five percent of the population in Uganda do not eat fish. The Bakigas, the Masais and Turkanas do not eat fish. But today the situation is changing because some people in these locations have started fish farming. This has resulted from the fact that these herdsmen are mixing up with other people of different cultures in schools, churches, parliaments, and in many other local community gatherings.

References

Allela, S. O. Development and Research of Aquaculture in Kenya. In Huisman, E. A. (ed.), Aquaculture Research in the African Region. Wegeninger, Netherlands: Pudoe, 1985.

Anon. For Fish Farmers, Newsletter from the Cooperatives Extension Service, Mississippi State University, October 25, 1980.

Anon. Programme - Fish Culture, 1971.

Anon. Fisheries in ACP States. The Courier 76, September-October, 1958.

Anon. Fisheries in ACP States. The Courier 66, June-July, 1955.

Anon. Spawn black bass in concrete race way. Aquaculture Magazine, 10(6A), 46, 1984.

Anon. Fisheries in ACP States. The Courier 85, May-June, 1971.

Anon. The Economics of Small-Scale Fish Farming in Western Nigeria. Paper prepared by the Fisheries Division, Ministry of Agriculture and Natural Resources, Ibadani, Nigeria, 1972.

Balarin, J. D. National Review for Aquaculture Development in Africa; Uganda, Mombasa: Kenya Baobab, Farm Ltd., 1985.

Balarin, J. D., and Haller, R. D. The Intensive Culture of Talapia in Tanks, Race Ways, and Cages. In Roberts, R. J., and Muir, J. F. (eds.), Recent Advances in Aquaculture. London: Croom Helm Ltd., 265-356, 1984.

Balarin, J. D., and Halton, J. Tilapia, A Guide to their Biology and Culture in Africa, 1979.

Boyd, C. E. Water Quality in Warm Water Fish Ponds, Agricultural Experiment Station, Auburn, Alabama, 1990.

Brannon, F. I. Mechanisms of Controlling Migration of Sockeye Salmon Fry, 1977.

Chemists, P. Tilapia and its Culture. FAO Fish. Bull., 8.1. 1955.

CIFA. A Preliminary Catalogue of Cultivated Fishes in Africa. CIFA, Working Party on
    Aquaculture. Nairobi: Kenya, 19-22, March, 1983.

Compton, J. Lin. Introduction to Agricultural Extension in the Developing Countries,
    Vol. 11, 1993.

Conrad, H. Aquaculture Development in Latin America. Boulder, CO: Westview Press,
    1990.

Cross, D. W., Pecker, E., and Insull, A. D. Central and Northern Regions Fish Farming
    Development Extension, Training and Research Project, Malawi, Landell Mills
    Association Ltd./Min. of Forestry and Natural Resources. 124 p., 1983.

De Moor, I., and Bruton, M. N. The Management of Invasive Aquatic Animals in South
    Africa: Ecosystems, FRD, CSTR, Pretoria, 1989.

FAO. A Study of Methodologies for Forecasting Aquaculture Development. Rome, 47 p.,
    1985.

FAO. Uganda, FAO Fish Cultivation Bull., 1(2), 1968.

FAO/ADB. Uganda: Review and Programming Mission. Rome: UNDP/FAO Mission
    Report, DP: DP/UGA 81/019: 226 p., 1980.

FAO. Aquaculture Aid Profiles: A Summary of Information on Aquaculture, 1982 Projects
    with External Components. Rome: FAO, ADOP/AD/82/5: 75 p., 1982.

FAO/UN. FAO Fish Culture Bull., 1(1): 11, 1968.

FAO/UNDP. Uganda: Review and Programming Mission. Rome: UNDP/FAO, Mission
    Report D.D. DP/UGA/81/019: 226 p., 1975.

Federal Government. Federal Department of Agriculture. Ibadan: Nigeria, 1971-72.

George, T. T. The History and Status of Fish Culture in Sudan and the Urgency of an Experimental Project for its Development into an Industry: A Review. FAO/CIFA Symposium on Aquaculture in Africa. Accra: Ghana, 1969.

Ginnally, S. Fish Farming in Tanks at Cachama. New York: Longman, Inc., 1990.

Gould, R. E. Progress of Fish Farming in Tanganyika Fisheries Series Pamphlet, No. 21, 1951.

Hofstede, A. E. Fish Farming in Sudan Khartoum: Annual Report, 1956-57.

Huet, M. Textbook of Fish Culture, 2nd ed. Oxford: Fish News Books, 1986.

Huet, M. Textbook of Fish Culture, Breeding and Cultivation of Pond Fish. Great Britain: Adland and Sons Ltd., Dorking, Survey, 1992.

Huisman, F. The Development of the East African Aquaculture. Nairobi: Government Press, 1985.

Ibrahim, K. H., and Lena, R. Growth Rates of I. Esculenta Graham and T. Zillii (Garvais) Undercultivation in Ponds at Nyagezi Tanzania. Program Symposium of Aquaculture Reservoirs of East and Central Africa, Kampala, 1972.

Ibrahim, K. H. Progress and Present Status of Aquaculture in Tanzania. FAO Symposium on Aquaculture in Africa. Dar-Salaam: 1970.

Kigeya, J. K. Problems and Prospects of Fish Culture Among Small Scale Farmers in Uganda: An Analysis of Technical, Social and Educational Dimensions. University of Wisconsin, Madison, 1995.

Knox, A. B. Helping Adults Learn. San Francisco: Jossey Bass Publishers, 1987.

Kaura, R., and El Bolock, A. R. Age, Growth and Survival of Tilapia Mossambica in Egyptian Ponds, Instruction, Ocean and Fish. Notes and Memoirs, UAR, No. 41, 1972.

Ling, S. W. Aquaculture in S.E. Asia: A Historical Overview. London: University Washington Press.

Maar, A. Carp Culture in Africa South of Sahara. In Symposium on Problems of Major Lakes, 1966.

Mechkat, A. Travel Report, Uganda. Rome: FAO, pp. 21, 1967.

Motabar, S. Fish Ponds Development in Sudan. Khartaum: Government Printing Press, 1973.

Pilley, T. V. R. Aquaculture Principles and Practices. United Nations, Rome, 1993.

Pilley, T. V. R. The Aquaculture; A Paper Presented at FAO Technical Conference on Aquaculture. Kyoto: Japan, 1976.

Pullin, R. S. V., et al. Choice of Tilapia Species for Aquaculture (Abstract) in Introduction to Symposium of Tilapia in Aquaculture. Nazareth, Israel, May 8-13, 1980.

Salaya, J. J., and Martinez, M. Estato Actual dela Acuiculture en Latin America. Paper presented at the First Symposium of Latin America Aquaculture Association. Maracay, Venezuela, 1977.

Semalcula, S. N., and Makoro, J. J. The Culture of Tilapia Species in Uganda. FAO Fish Representative 44, pp. 161-164, 1967.

Singh, S. B. Rapid Survey of the Kidatu and Mtera Areas for Planning Fisheries Development Under the Great Ruaha Power Project. Tanzania: Fisheries Division, 11 p., 1979.

Smith, L. J., and Peterson, S. Aquaculture Development in Less Developed Countries Social, Economic and Political Problems. Boulder, CO: Westview Press, 1982.

Suna. The Fisheries Hydrobiological Research Section, Introduction of Carp Culture for Sudan Ponds and Reservoirs. Suna Daily Bulletin, Vol. 1431, No. 7, 1975.

Swift, S. R. Estado Actually de Desarrollo del Acuiculture en Latino America. Paper Presented at the Fish Symposium of Latin American Aquaculture Association. Maracay, Venezuela, 1977.

WHO. Conference on the Safety of Biological Agents for Arthropod Control. VBC/73.1, 1973.

Vincke, M. M. J. La Vulgarisation en Milieu Rural en Afrique Centrale, 1982.

Wakabi, K. (Mrs.). Personal Interview at Kajansi Experimental Station, 1993.

Wyrand, V., Hacht, Y. S., and Britz, M. Acquaculture in South Africa. Wanger Manufacturing Inc., 1992.